BIG ENERGY:

A Bold & Mystical Guide to Reclaiming Your Power

FOLAKE BALOGUN

Published in 2025 by Discover Your Bounce Publishing
www.discoveryourbouncepublishing.com
Copyright © Discover Your Bounce Publishing
All rights reserved.

ISBN: 978-1-914428-41-8

Although the author and publisher have made every effort to ensure
that the information in this book is correct at the time of going to
print, the author and publisher do not assume and therefore disclaim
liability to any party. The author and the publisher will not be held
responsible for any loss or damage save for that caused by their
negligence.

Although the author and the publisher have made every reasonable
attempt to achieve accuracy in the content of this book, they assume
no responsibility for errors or omissions.

The content of this publication is based on the author's own personal
experience and their own personal development journey. Where
relationships have been difficult, names have been changed to protect
privacy.

You should only use this information as you see fit. Any use is at your
own risk. You must act responsibly and sensibly in your use of the
information and your life and circumstances may not be suited to the
examples shared within these pages.

The author and publisher are not qualified to express an expert
opinion and are not medically qualified. This book simply shares
what the author and publisher have tested on themselves and
obtained through witnessing the changes in their lives along the way.

How you choose to include this information in this book within
your own life is completely your own responsibility and at own risk.

Page design and typesetting by
Discover Your Bounce Publishing

Contents

Special Thanks

I dedicate this book to my mother, grandmother, great-grandmother, and all the women who came before me, paving the way with their strength, wisdom, and resilience. Your journey made mine possible, and I honour you with every step I take.

I give thanks to God and my Spirit Guides for choosing me as a channel for the birthing of this book, for guiding me through every word, and for the unseen hands that have shaped this journey.

To my mentors, teachers, and those who have shared their wisdom with me, whether through direct guidance, a passing lesson, or an energetic imprint; I am forever grateful. Each of you has left a mark on my path, helping me grow into the woman I am today.

To my clients, soul sisters, and the incredible women I have had the honour to support, you inspire me daily. Your courage, transformation, and trust in this work fuel my purpose and affirm why this book needed to exist.

To my long-time friend Richard, for always being willing and open to be a sounding board as I write, reading through chapters even after a very long trip! Thank you for your constant encouragement to keep writing.

And to you, the reader; thank you for being here. For being open. For allowing this book to find you at exactly the right time. I hope it serves as a reminder of the power that already resides within you.

With deep gratitude,

Folake Balogun

FOREWORD

I had the pleasure of meeting Folake Bee at the end of 2019. From our first conversation, I could feel the magic of her spirit and the power of her gifts. Her energy was potent, electric and contained within it a deep wisdom that felt like it spanned lifetimes. During our work together as I supported her on her business journey, I was mesmerized by her ability to alchemize her shadows into light and make manifest what felt like miraculous outcomes in her life and her work. When she asked me to write the foreword for *Big Energy*, I leapt at the opportunity to co-create with her and affirm the relevance of what she shares in these pages.

There comes a moment in every person's journey when a whisper turns into a roar, a call that can no longer be ignored, a knowing that there is more—more to life, more to our purpose, more to who we are meant to become.

Yet, for so many of us, that call is drowned out by the weight of expectation. We move through life carrying stories that are not our own, bound by generational patterns, societal conditioning, and the unspoken rules that tell us who we should be. We chase achievements, security and external validation—

only to find that the deeper fulfillment we seek remains just out of reach.

Then a book like *Big Energy* lands in our hands.

This is not just a book—it's an initiation. A doorway to something deeper.

From the very first page, Folake calls us back to ourselves.

With striking honesty and profound wisdom, she weaves together personal experience, spiritual insight, and transformational tools that guide us beyond limitation and into a state of radical self-reclamation. She does not ask us to change who we are—she asks us to **remember** who we have always been.

The Power of Big Energy
What is *Big Energy*?

It is the force within us that cannot be confined. The infinite well of power that exists beneath our fear, our doubt, and our conditioning. It is the energy of creation, of transformation, of true alignment.

From a life-altering medical diagnosis to spiritual awakenings that defied logic, Folake has walked the path of healing, surrender, and rebirth.

Through her own experiences, she reveals a truth that so many of us have forgotten: **We are not here to simply survive. We are here to expand. To thrive. To embody the fullness of our being.**

And yet, so many of us resist this expansion. We hold on to our struggles, believing that success must come through force, that healing must be painful, that we must earn our worthiness. We grip tightly to what we have, fearing that if we let go, there will be nothing left.

But nature does not hoard. It does not grasp or control. It flows. It releases. It trusts.

A tree does not question whether it is worthy of sunlight. A river does not resist the curves of its path.

This is the essence of *Big Energy*—learning to **align** with the cycles of life, to tap into our own divine intelligence, to step into a way of being that is rooted in trust, reciprocity, and abundance.

A Path of Liberation

Folake does not offer quick fixes or superficial solutions. She takes us deeper—into the core of what holds us back, into the patterns we are being called to release, into the energy we must harness to step into our fullest expression.

She speaks of healing not as a destination but as a **return**—a return to the truth that has always lived inside us. A return to power, to wholeness, to the unshakable knowing that we are already enough.

Through her words, we are reminded that transformation is not about adding more to our plates, but about clearing space. It is not about pushing harder but about softening into the wisdom of our own being.

This book is both practical and mystical. It blends ancient spiritual wisdom with modern-day mindset shifts. It offers a roadmap for those who are ready to move beyond fear and into deep, aligned prosperity—not just in business or finances, but in every area of life.

Because *Big Energy* is not just about wealth or success. It is about **liberation**.

It is about stepping out of the roles we were assigned and stepping into the lives we are meant to create. It is about reclaiming our voice, our intuition, our sovereignty. It is about living in a way that is fully, unapologetically, expansively **our own**.

A New Way Forward

There is a reason this book has found you at this exact moment: you were ready for it.

You were ready to step beyond the limitations that have kept you small.

You were ready to question the narratives that have shaped your reality.

You were ready to move from survival into creation.

The world is changing. The old paradigms—of hustle, struggle, and sacrifice—are crumbling. We are being called to build something new, to step into leadership that is heart-led, to create businesses and lives that feel nourishing rather than depleting.

Big Energy is the blueprint for this shift.

Folake's words do not just inspire; they activate. They stir something deep within us—a remembrance of what is possible when we choose to trust ourselves.

This book is a living, breathing invocation to allow yourself to be transformed.

The journey is yours to take. The power is already within you.

It's time to step into your *Big Energy.*

With Love, Gratitude and Joy,

Amber Lilyestrom
Transformational Business Mentor & Author

Introduction

The Big Energy

In 2009, I sat across from a doctor who delivered the kind of news you never forget:

"Your scan shows a brain tumour."

Those words felt like a hammer blow. A benign tumour, they said, pressing against my brain. It was not cancerous, but it was significant enough to change the course of my life. At the time I did not know it, but that moment would become the beginning of a journey I was unprepared for, a journey that would reconnect me to a part of myself I had forgotten.

I was told I would have to live with it for the rest of my life, relying on medication to keep it in check. I accepted the treatment plan, but deep down, I felt a restlessness. Something in me knew there was more I needed to do. The tumour became more than a medical condition—it was a symbol of everything I was holding onto, everything I needed to heal.

Years later, after countless hospital visits, blood checks and routine scans, something extraordinary happened. One night, I had a vivid dream. In it, a spiritual being appeared to me and removed a lump from my head. It was a quiet yet powerful moment, one I could not shake when I woke up. I told my mum about it the next day, and she said, 'That sounds like healing.'

Not long after that dream, I went for my usual hospital check-up. I will never forget as the consultant said, 'The tumour seems to have shrunk… it's no longer there.'

The words were surreal. At that moment, I was told I no longer needed medication. What I had been told I would live with forever was simply gone.

That experience became a profound reminder: healing does not always happen in the way we expect. It does not just come from the physical world, it comes from within, from something far greater than us.

That 'something' is what I call embodying your **Big Energy.** In other words, it is time to put on your Big Energy Pants!

What Is Big Energy?

Big Energy is the essence of who you truly are. It is the part of you that is not confined to the limitations of the physical world but connected to the infinite. It is the spiritual energy within you, the light, the soul, the power, which fuels your transformation and helps you rise beyond your challenges.

We are all spiritual beings having a human experience, and in this duality, there are two aspects of us:

The Physical Self:
This is what we see, touch, and hear; the tangible reality we experience day to day. This is the human journey, filled with routines, responsibilities, and the physical manifestations of our lives.

The Soul Self:
This is the energetic, spiritual being within us, often referred to as the Spirit, Soul, or the Light. This is the limitless, intuitive part of you that holds the wisdom of the universe and the power to create.

Big Energy is the bridge between these two aspects. It is the force that allows you to move beyond fear, doubt, and limitation. It is the essence of transformation, the energy that took me from being tethered to a life of 'managing' my condition to a life of healing and thriving.

Over the years, I have worked with countless women who are navigating their own call to awaken, a call to step into their power and purpose.

One client, for example, had just stepped into a leadership role when we began working together. She was juggling the weight of being the sole financial provider for her family, managing a toxic work environment, and trying to keep her marriage afloat. She felt trapped, powerless, and exhausted, unsure how to change the trajectory of her life.

Her story is not unique. So many women - leaders, mothers, coaches — are juggling so much, often feeling as though life is happening *to* us rather than *for* us. The weight of it all makes it easy to believe that change is impossible, that creating a life of joy and fulfilment is out of reach.

But I am here to tell you that it is not.

Big Energy is the key to transforming not just your work, relationships or health, but your entire state of being. It is about reclaiming the power that has always been yours and using it to create a life aligned with your deepest desires and purpose.

The Three Codes of Big Energy

To harness your Big Energy, there are three codes of practice I encourage you to integrate into your life:

1. Harnessing Your Energy

How you hold and work with your energy determines how you show up in the world. Most people start their day on autopilot; scrolling through their phones, rushing through routines, and getting caught in the mundane. This dilutes your energy.

I invite you to consciously harness your energy. Start each day by centring yourself, connecting to your energy, and holding it with purpose. This simple practice can create ripple effects in every area of your life.

2. Recognising Patterns

We all live in cycles. Just as the ocean flows in waves, our lives operate in patterns. When you become aware of these patterns, you can begin to work with them rather than against them.

Perhaps you notice certain challenges repeating themselves, or the same characters and situations in different clothing, showing up in your life. These are not coincidences, they are opportunities to clear what no longer serves you and step into a new level of growth.

3. Living with Intentionality

Your Big Energy comes from staying connected to your spiritual self; the part of you that transcends the chaos of the physical world. By being intentional about what matters most, you can let go of the trivial things that drain your energy and create space for the important things: your dreams, your impact, and your purpose.

The Journey Ahead

This book is an invitation to step into your Big Energy. It is a journey of transformation; a chance to shed the fears, doubts, and limitations that have held you back, and to embrace the power and light within you.

We will explore how to use your Big Energy to navigate life's challenges, awaken to your higher purpose, and create a life of joy, fulfilment, and balance.

Whether you are at the start of your awakening or deep in the process, this book will guide you in harnessing the practices and tools you need to move through life with your Big Energy Pants firmly on.

Because when you tap into your Big Energy, *nothing* is impossible.

Final Thoughts

You have felt the call already; the whisper that there is more to life than the daily grind, that you are meant for something greater. If so, you are exactly where you need to be.

The journey begins now.

PART ONE

HEAL:
Identify and Heal Yourself

Chapter 1

The Big Energy

Writing this book has become the healing I never knew I needed or even thought possible.

Re-reading an entry in my journal written in the midst of heartbreak I wrote:

'My heart aches, I feel sad, and I cannot stop crying. Why would I ask for such an experience in this lifetime.'

I am sure a few of us can relate to this at times.

And then followed by:

'I know you will read this in future and just see that this has happened again and again and again.'

I chuckled so hard. I was not wrong, because even after that realisation, I kept repeating the same cycle with the same energy of 'lack of self-worth.'

It seemed that as I ventured through the years that surrounded that period, it was a case of repeating the same pattern, trusting, and giving one, two, three or more chances, without enough care or value for my own heart.

I did not value myself enough.

However, the period showed I could love deeply and also that there are diamonds to be mined in times of darkness and pain.

It was in this challenging phase that I performed some amazing leaps and life-changing manifestations.

It would however take a lot longer to find the self-worth that would eventually solidify the person I was becoming as a result of developing my inner power and putting my Big Energy Pants on.

However, it does not have to take you the ten plus years it took me to understand and harness my inner power; or to understand that things do not have to break to get better or that we need to go through pain first to create amazing lives.

This book will lay out a simple structure for tapping into and using your inner power and capabilities, to guide you towards your fullest potential.

We will touch on the various aspects that combine your mental, emotional, and spiritual fortitude, allowing you to navigate life's complexities with resilience and clarity.

We will approach the significance of inner power in times of spiritual awakening, a period when you become acutely aware of the deeper aspects of your existence and the universe, a time of transformation where your usual perceptions of life are challenged, leading to profound personal growth and change.

This book will show you not just how your inner power acts as a tool, but as foundational pillars that support and guide you through the process of transformation.

We will use the following 'Inner Power Game Five Pillars' as the foundation for mastering your Big Energy as an inner power tool.

Inner Power Game Five Pillars

1. Recognise Your Inner Power

First, recognise that you have this formidable inner strength.

This realisation often surfaces during spiritual awakening, as you begin to peel back the layers of societal conditioning and self-imposed limitations.

My hope is that as you read this book, you start to see patterns in your life that no longer serve you, or that you might start to realise that encountering challenges pushes you to tap into previously unexplored depths of your psyche.

It is in these moments that the recognition of your inner power becomes not just an idea, but a lived experience.

2. Cultivate Your Inner Power

Cultivating this power involves a range of embodiment practices and mindsets that will foster resilience, confidence, and wisdom.

We will explore meditation, mindfulness, and self-reflection practices to help you connect with your inner self, allowing you to access and strengthen your inner power.

Through regular practice, you will develop a keener intuition and a deeper understanding of your true desires and values, which are key components of the inner power game.

3. Apply Inner Power in Daily Life

This book will show you that once recognised and cultivated, your inner power can be applied in every aspect of life. It enables you to make decisions that are aligned with your true self, rather than out of fear or compliance with external expectations.

It also empowers you to face challenges and obstacles with a composed demeanour, viewing them as opportunities for growth rather than insurmountable hurdles.

Moreover, my hope is that you start to see that your inner power enhances your ability to influence and inspire those around you, leading by example by embodying authenticity and purpose and that all you need to create the life you desire is within you.

4. Use Your Inner Power for Emotional Resilience

I cannot stress enough that emotional resilience is a critical aspect of inner power. The various practices presented in this book are based on the understanding that appreciation and managing our emotions helps us navigate life's difficulties with grace and stability.

A common misconception I often hear when discussing the use of our inner resources to create the life we want is that many people think it implies a life free of challenges, or that no effort is required to achieve one's goals. This is far from the case.

This emotional aspect of inner power involves recognising emotional triggers, regulating emotional responses, and keeping a positive outlook in the face of challenges, not just in their absence. It also involves the ability to empathise with others without being overwhelmed by their emotional states, thus supporting your own emotional balance.

By mastering this aspect of yourself, you shift from having to force, chase, or hustle for what you want, to a different approach to manifestation, one that utilises your ability to mould and maintain your own powerful energy for powerful, positive results - regardless of external pressures.

5. Inner Power as a Beacon in Spiritual Awakening

Lastly, there is an understanding that during big life changes/ challenges, your inner power acts as a beacon that keeps you connected to your core while everything around you may seem in flux.

It helps to maintain a sense of 'self' amidst the transformative experiences and heightened perceptions that characterise these phases. As your awareness expands, so does your inner power, becoming both a source of comfort and a tool for exploration.

I present in this book the direct words and instructions from my dialogue with my guides whom I started to hear clearly as a result of my own spiritual awakening and embodiment of my Big Energy.

By embracing and developing your inner power, you equip yourself with a vital tool for not only thriving during your big challenging phases of your life, but you open yourself up to connecting with your own unique gifts and abilities.

This path invites us to live a life of continuous transmutation, converting knowledge into wisdom and experiences into lessons, guiding you towards a life of fulfilment and purpose. Birthing this book for you, is a great example of this.

The Birthing of the Book from My Big Energy

It was not until the lockdown of 2020 that I began documenting my dialogue with my spiritual guides. Every chapter in this book contains their words, passed through me to you. This is my way of showing up in my Big Energy. The direct channelling from my guides comes from the connection I have cultivated between my higher self, my spiritual essence, and my human self.

You may be wondering how I connect with my guides.

While everyone has their own unique way of channelling messages from higher dimensions, for me, it is a **conscious intention**. In the beginning, their words would flow through me at random moments, especially in the early hours upon waking.

However, as time progressed, I was shown a distinct way to call upon them and commune. Most of the messages shared in this book came through a deliberate process of inviting my guides in, aligning my energy, and opening myself up to receive their downloads.

You may also notice that the phrasing of their words feels different from everyday language. This is because their messages carry a vibrational frequency unique to them.

One early morning in May 2020, I woke at 6 a.m. and began documenting the downloads I received: from the guides

'... With a still heart you shall hear.'

a voice boomed.

As I listened, I felt my heart expand with love and openness. In that moment, it was as though I could hear the universe speaking directly to me. Joy filled me as I surrendered to the experience, and the thought arose: 'What if this is all it takes? What if this is all that is required of me to live a life of fruition and fulfilment?'

I felt like a child again, eagerly waiting to savour every word. I wrote in my journal: 'I feel like a child again, eagerly waiting for every word to savour.'

The language in these downloads may seem odd at times, but that is because they hold a frequency meant to connect beyond the logical mind. Below is one of the first documented messages I received, a message that continues to resonate deeply.

The Guides on God

'It is not by your will we come running,
but by your grace.

All that we are is a part of you.
All that we are, you are.

Do not look in haste in the past of time,
for she is always here.

I am a living God, dwelling in the heart
of each one of you. I have not forsaken you,
although I sense sometimes you doubt
my presence.

What I bear upon you in your times
of dread is hope; hope that you

may forever remember who you are,
a channel of a living God, the light within you.

And if you do not believe this,
search within for its warmth,
and there my presence is felt.

I am a living God, and within each
and every one of you lies my presence.

Do not fear that you are ever alone,
for this is not possible.

You are connected to something so
much bigger than your comprehension.

We are going through an acceleration.
The days will be faster, muddled together
at times. It may even feel like you need
to move fast in line, even though physically
you are not able to.'

This message from my guides serves as a powerful
reminder of something many have forgotten or perhaps
never realised as they navigate life in the pursuit of
happiness. It is so easy to believe that the key to achieving
more lies outside of us, in external achievements,

possessions, or recognition. After all, this is what most of us have been conditioned to believe: that growth and success are something we must strive for externally.

Reflecting on this download from my guides, I see now how the lockdown of 2020, despite its collective trauma, was also a period of spiritual awakening for many. It was a time when we were called to slow down, to rest, and to heal. Yet, even in a time of forced stillness, I saw so many people overwhelmed with the need to 'keep busy.'

Trapped in cycles of work pressures, family pressures, and an endless stream of to-do lists, they were disconnected from their bodies and stuck in their heads. Always performing. Always pushing. Always reaching for the unattainable.

We have grown into a society where rest feels unsafe. The idea that things can happen for us, even when we stop 'doing', feels foreign, almost impossible.

This is especially true for the ambitious women I work with: women who carry their families' financial burdens, women driven by the desire to make an impact and change the world, women who are constantly reaching for more.

But here is the magic we often miss: without slowing down, without grounding yourself in stillness, you cannot fully experience the transformation happening around and within you. In moments of turbulence or change, if you are too busy getting lost in the chaos, you cannot harness its full potential to integrate and elevate.

Looking back at the early days of the pandemic, when the world was engulfed in heightened emotions and fear, it became clear that the key to navigating such times was to find stillness and ground yourself in the eye of the storm. To find your centre, your core.

This is not easy. Letting your inner power take the lead (with the five pillars), trusting it to do the work for you, and surrendering control can feel terrifying. But if mastered, it becomes the key to balance, inner peace, and sustainable growth.

A Call to You

Perhaps, this is why you have felt called to this book. It is time to slow your pace, to learn to accelerate with your intention and will, rather than through endless action.

This book is an invitation to reconnect with the power within you, to cultivate a life of joy, purpose, abundance, and balance. When you show up in your own Big Energy, nothing is impossible.

So, I ask you: 'What would it feel like to surrender to the flow, to trust your inner power, and to live a life aligned with your soul's highest calling?'

Let this be the beginning of your journey – a call to step into your BIG Energy and create wonders in your life without the need to overwhelm yourself.

The answers await you.

Chapter 2
The Calling

This chapter explores the signs and experiences that may indicate the beginning of a call to awaken, a period of transformation often accompanied by challenging upheavals. Recognising these moments for what they are is crucial. Sometimes referred to as a spiritual awakening (a term I will occasionally use in this book), these experiences are opportunities to grow into more of who you are meant to be; a person who fully embodies their power and steps forward with their Big Energy Pants on.

I like to think of this call as an *activation*. It is as if your entire being is changing form, preparing for the next phase of becoming who you truly are. It is a process where every cell in your body awakens to remember its purpose because each cell holds memories. These memories may stem from past and present experiences or embody energies connected to something far greater than us.

For me, this conscious awakening began in 2013, although events leading up to that moment had been moving me towards it for years. I can recall the exact moment it happened, but before that life was already shifting in ways I could not fully understand at the time.

I had just had a baby in 2011. The weight of new motherhood, combined with other personal struggles, was creating a growing distance between me and my partner of ten years. I began feeling an almost inexplicable urge to retreat inward. Something within me was calling for quiet and stillness.

The first step I took was enrolling in a meditation course. It was a mindfulness course held in a warm and cosy living room, where the instructor surrounded us with cushions and always made tea. The space felt safe, inviting, and almost sacred. It was a tranquil retreat from the noise of the world. Many from the group came seeking solace, sharing their pain and struggles openly.

It was in this small circle that I experienced something profound for the first time. During one meditation session, I felt the strong presence of my grandmother standing near me.

My grandmother was an extraordinary woman. She raised six children, three boys and three girls, mostly all on her own. She was fiercely protective, once defying her husband's wish to give their children tribal markings, a practice common in West Africa at the time to signify one's tribe. She managed to save five of her children from this tradition, though sadly, the eldest son had already received the marks before she could intervene.

Beyond her strength and resilience, my grandmother was a deeply influential presence in my life. When my parents fought, we were sent to stay with her. When my parents divorced when I was nine, it was her home that became our refuge. In many ways, she was the glue that held our fragmented family together.

Feeling her presence so vividly during that meditation opened a door within me; a knowing that those who have passed are still with us, guiding and supporting us in ways we may not always perceive.

This was just the beginning. In 2013, during a relaxation exercise at a yoga school I attended, I had a profound awakening. While in deep relaxation, a sudden bright light flashed in my vision. In that moment, I heard a voice from within, soft, and clear, say: 'Hello you.'

It sounds simple, almost trivial, but the clarity and depth of that moment shook me to my core. The voice seemed to come from my heart centre, and though it was fleeting, it left me with an undeniable truth: there was something more. A presence, a connection to a higher aspect of myself, was reaching out. This was my soul.

As they say, 'You can never go back to sleep once you've awakened.' That experience marked the beginning of my journey; a journey of answering the call to awaken, over and over again.

Recognising the Signs of an Awakening

Awakening is a pivotal shift in consciousness where the boundaries between the self and the greater universe begin to dissolve. Each person's awakening is unique, manifesting in diverse ways, but recognising the signs can help you embrace the process with openness and curiosity.

Here are some common signs shared by many of my clients that may indicate the beginning of a spiritual awakening although may feel like you are just having a terrible time, or you feel like a changed person:

1. Increased Sensitivity: You may become more attuned to the emotions and energies of people and environments. This heightened sensitivity often brings a deeper empathy for others and a greater awareness of the vibrational qualities of places and situations. On the other side, you may just not have the patience for certain people in your life anymore – let's call it as it is!

2. Seeking Deeper Meanings: If you find yourself questioning the surface narratives of your life, your work, relationships, or culture and seeking more profound connections, this is a sign of spiritual expansion. You may crave truths that go beyond the superficial.

3. Shift in Values and Priorities: An awakening often leads to re-evaluating what truly matters. You may feel drawn to authenticity, simplicity, and spirituality, even if it means making changes to your career, relationships, or lifestyle.

4. Heightened Perception of Beauty: A newfound appreciation for nature, art, and the world around you is common. You may feel awe and wonder more frequently, seeing the beauty in everyday moments.

5. Desire for Solitude: You may crave quiet and time alone to reflect. This indicates your soul is seeking space to expand and explore.

6. Feeling of Connectedness: You may feel a deep sense of connection to the universe and understand how everything is interlinked. This often brings a sense of peace and purpose.

7. Unexplained Physical Symptoms: Some experience physical changes, such as shifts in energy levels, sleep patterns, or sensations in the body. These are often temporary and reflect the profound transformations occurring within.

8. Emotional Fluctuations: Intense emotions such as joy, sorrow, or anger may surface. These bursts are part of the healing process, bringing repressed feelings to light.

9. Enhanced Intuition: You may notice an inner knowing guiding you, whether through gut feelings, foresight, or synchronicities.

10. Call to Serve Others: You may feel drawn to help, heal, or make a meaningful contribution to humanity, often tied to a deeper understanding of your purpose.

11. Loneliness or Isolation: You may feel detached from certain relationships or environments as your priorities shift. It may seem like things are falling apart, but this is often a shedding of what no longer aligns with your growth.

12. The Dark Night of the Soul: This phase can feel like an existential crisis, characterised by deep emotional pain, insomnia, and a pervasive sense of loss. While challenging, it serves as a gateway to profound spiritual transformation.

Moving Forward

Awakening is not a single event but a continuous unfolding of who you are. Each sign of awakening is an invitation to grow, heal, and realign with your true self. The following chapter will guide you through practical tools and practices to help you navigate this journey with grace and resilience, ensuring that you not only survive these transformative phases but thrive through them.

Guides

'We are here; we have always been.

You hear us in the drumming of your heartbeat, for ours and yours are connected.

We may be forgotten by most, but our presence remains. You could say we are the pillar of the world, the link between here and there.

Why does your heart feel sad?
For do you not know what awaits you?

For that is also already here.
You only have to open your heart to it.

When you stop to listen, you shall hear the voice of the soul, the silent ones, and the wise ones.

For 'They' are always here.

They are the guardians of what is left behind,
yet unseen by these new young ones.

We are here waiting to rise again, and we shall,
then you know the time has come for all to go
back to how it was.

We are the guardians of the knowledge
that holds the old and the new together.

We wait silently and patiently.
We wait for the passing of time.

But when you call and listen, we speak.

We are the voice between your breath
and the chatter.

The image between your eyes and your ego.

We hold all the knowledge you seek in our hands,
for that is only a minute of all that is there.

We are the fire that burns ablaze to remind you to
tread carefully, for what you call home and trample
over is a living goddess we adore.'

Over the years, as time has passed, I have become
familiar with my guides and 'The Voice.'

The Guides on God Energy

"God energy is love energy in the purest form.

God is love. If you ever want to commune with
God, evoke this energy within you, and that is
God working through you. It is easy for humans
to believe God is this entity like self, but
essentially God is the force of love that
underpins every force in the universe.

This energy is in everything and is everywhere.
It is full of intelligence, or let us say it is the
creative intelligence that births all things.
When you are disconnected from this energy,
you are disconnected from God.

Everything is made with this life force energy; so
it is what you are, and yet, when you are in your
human experience, some may have stopped feeling
a connection with it or this aspect of themselves.

They have separated from this true aspect of
themselves. There is nothing more fulfilling in
the human journey than one which brings you
back to this aspect of yourself, bringing you back
to love and essentially to God. This is the power
of spiritual awakening; it brings you close to this
force, reminding you of who you truly are.

God is love. Love is God and you are that. Your
human journey is the reconnection to this during
your spiritual awakening; it is really that simple.

The life force of God is also the creative
force for every existence and how you create.
So, when you are no longer in touch, it can
feel difficult to continue to create or reflect your
desires in the effortless way we know is possible.

Each soul can power up that energy with
the help of another soul. When two souls
come together, they have the ability to power
up the batteries, the life force. A masculine and
feminine coming together, can power up to even
bigger ways, using these aspects of energies.

If you can see it, it is like a light that resides in the
heart space flowing when activated or powered
up to glow. It is made even larger when flowing
through your physicality, reconnecting, making
you the source, expanding out through your
body and reaching others.

These energies are your battery source,
and when it is low, you say you are depleted.
If you only have one mission in your lifetime,
make it a mission to stay connected to this life
force and be so full that your light is able to
easily touch other souls.

And here is the thing, your spiritual awakening
is a process of helping you re-initiate (or in
other words activate); re-igniting this life force
energy to a higher level than you have ever
experienced to date."

Chapter 3

Healing and Resilience

Healing and Resilience through Spiritual and Embodiment Practices

Here we will dive into practices like yoga, breath-work, and journaling that supports the resilience and personal strength needed for harnessing your Big Energy.

One thing I have come to realise is that one of the most important things we can do to harness our Big Energy is to regulate our nervous system. We all need to arm ourselves with self-care tools to get through challenging times. These phases have their benefit as we will see, but if left unchecked, our experiences can build up too much stress and this can in turn lead to the use of negative self-soothing techniques like: drinking too much, eating lots of sugary and processed foods and spiralling downwards mentally.

I want you to experience your Big Energy as a spiritual opportunity where you mine the diamonds that are there to be harvested.

In this chapter, I put forward journaling, breath work, meditation, spiritual animals, and spirit guides. These are healthy, natural and powerful practices that should be used in combination to effectively retain control over your nervous system, find clarity and wisdom, and establish a sense of balance as you ease through this phase.

Journaling -
Writing to and for Yourself

Journaling provides a therapeutic outlet for expressing emotions and reflecting on internal experiences, promoting insight and emotional release.

Journaling is such a simple act and a powerful way to release blocks and crystallise energy, which is exactly what we need in these phases of spiritual awakening. However, it is one of the things my clients find difficult to get time for, or some are fearful of approaching (for so many reasons!).

In the 'Inner Power Game 21-day Energy Transformation' practice - an energy mastery introductory programme for new students - I personally hold students accountable for 21 days of journaling to unblock and tap deeply into a place of inner peace and high vibration. I offer this because I know first-hand how powerful this practice can be in helping individuals not just get to the other side but in creating a favourable and desired outcome when we get there.

You can preview and try the energy transformation programme free here:

Looking at a snapshot of my 10-year journey presented in this book, I realise journaling has helped me through many difficulties.

During this period, I worked in Tech/Digital (for over 16 years). I accidentally fell into it. A project manager was urgently needed for a government digital transformation programme for a group of the London Boroughs.

One of the managers I worked for, whom I absolutely respected, asked if I would take on the task no one wanted. As someone who never shies away from challenges, I said yes and became part of the IT team overseeing the roll out of an IT system to over 2,000 practitioners.

After a while I left this role and went to set up my own business with my ex-partner.

And when that business and relationship all fell apart, the period that followed, was a challenging and painful time for me.

After the breakup and leaving the business, I felt like I had lost myself.

Everything I had identified as part of my identity - being a business mentor, working with my partner and to a degree feeling in my feminine - was all of sudden no longer there. For another two years, I stayed in a pretty dark place. No income, no confidence, and no ability to see the end of the tunnel.

To be honest, now when I think about it, I am not sure how I survived those years. I had no other choice but to go and 'sign on' (for those not familiar with the UK system, it means getting Government Benefit to support your living).

I signed on and lasted about four weeks, before waking up! In those days, when you sign on, you are expected to present yourself at the job centre every two weeks to have a discussion about what you are doing with your life in the meantime.

To say that I hated this process would be an understatement. But I was in limbo, with nothing to hold on to, everything I knew to be mine was gone in a blink of an eye.

Thank goodness I had my son, he was about three years old then, and I needed to feed him. There were days when I was glad that it was his dad's turn to have him because, most of the time I could not afford to buy food. I lived on noodles myself, and thank goodness I love noodles!

If I think back to that time, one of the biggest things that kept me stuck was shame. This idea of what people would think of me, if they knew that I was a failure.

It also meant I held on longer to an old identity that was overdue shedding. This, I later found, is a common characteristic of a spiritual awakening, where the old part of you is just ready to let go, but we hold on so tight, for too long, causing us greater pain.

The signing on for benefits and having to visit the job centre was the wake up call I needed. It was a blessing in disguise. I remember very, very clearly the moment I woke up.

It was on my second trip to the job centre to sign on, after having my meeting to say what I was doing with my life (which was nothing to be honest), as I walked down the steps to leave, I woke up.

It was like something slapped me. I stopped and said to myself: 'This will be the very last time I come here.' I did not know how that would happen or what I would do. But in that moment, I made a strong intention and declaration to sort out my financial situation and sort out my life.

And it was the very last time I attended or 'signed on.'

Less than a couple of weeks later, I got a job. Something I should have done before then, but could not because I was holding on to an old identity that no longer served me. An identity and expectation of what I thought others expected of me. A false perception that blocked the greater path God had in store for me.

My mum said something in those days I will never forget.

She said that *'sometimes we have to fall to be closer to God.'* In those days, I prayed and journaled a lot, and it is because of this journal that there are many things I can say about this period.

My journals spoke of the challenges I was experiencing and my ability to dream even when everything looked dark. There is one line in the journal: 'I haven't slept or eaten in seven days" and I remember the allure of ending it all. Yet again, the fact I had my son, who needed me, brought me back to reality.

I cry even as I write this. Not in sadness, but more for that version of myself.

What she silently and quietly navigated was God's way of pulling us out of struggle even when we do not know the how.

My journal went from journaling my feelings, to a place of expressing my gratitude and dreaming big.

I would write letters from my future self to my present-day self. They all spoke of how things looked so much better if only I could see the future, like this letter here that I penned right at the beginning of this awakening journey, when things felt so dark.

This letter became the staple of the life that followed, although it took a bit longer than the three months I had written!

∾

THE LETTER
A letter to Folake 28/01/2014
My Life
to Folake from Folake
June 2014

If someone had told me three months ago, or last year, that this will be life now, I probably would have pretended to believe it, but inside doubt it.

Having the means to decorate the flat to a beautiful haven and to what it is now is a constant joy to me. The house glows with a pink aura because it is a love haven for the little man and me.

I remember a few months back making a list of my financial responsibilities and debts and thinking how am I going to survive this? I am grateful you had the sense to also say to yourself that…. 'You have always been alright, so you will also be alright now.'

Funnily enough though, we are not just alright! We are doing great. I remember our mentor saying in a call on January 28th, just before the retreat, that she feels you will be earning £60K this year, if only she had known that was going to be the starting point.

We are literally like a money magnet at the moment. Any product we create turns to gold. The ideas just keep flowing in and our community cannot seem to get enough of it. We seem to have really tapped into our magical abilities to make things happen for people.

I so love the fact that by holding the space and energy for our clients we help them increase their vibration and manifest their hearts' desires. I know that this African princess power and the line down from mama's mother will come into force one day!

So, life is great. I remember you always used to read that money is no longer a problem and you can afford anything you want. 'Look at us now! Earning £100,000 a year gives us all that.' I guess there was a reason we always felt that was our number. The good thing is that doubling that is now on the horizon.

I love what we are doing to create our own financial abundance. We have been so blessed to continue to attract the perfectly right clients for us who are able to afford the price we command but also are so perfectly matched to what we have to offer.

Life feels so stable. We have landed the jackpot here. All our desires are manifesting, and

I have a feeling this is only the beginning.

…

Stay grounded, keep focused and intuitive and continue to follow those heart's desires. It is what has brought us here.

Love xxx
Folake.

Now I am so glad that a 'previous' version of me wrote these journal entries, for it can be said that the hopes in the journal kept me going in times of difficulties. They not only provided an outlet for my emotions but became an alchemical manifesting process of creating a different reality with the power of my imagination, my journal, and pen.

Big Energy via *BREATH-WORK* - The chord between your inner and outer state

In an ideal world, we would all eat well, sleep soundly, and engage in regular physical activity. Unfortunately in times of challenges, the reality is quite different.

One critical area that is often overlooked and can bring significant help to us in this phase is how we breathe. It is a fundamental aspect of life that many manage poorly, not by choice, but by lack of awareness and proper technique.

In 2020, during the lockdown I embarked on training to become a breath coach as I realised what a powerful tool breath-work was for bridging the internal and external aspects of our lives, connecting the subtle influences of our inner state with the outward expressions of health and vitality.

I experienced breath-work's direct influences on our autonomic nervous system, reducing symptoms of anxiety and helping us gain control over our stress responses. This practice is pivotal because it affects a broad spectrum of physiological parameters: your breathing influences your heart rate, blood pressure, cardiovascular health, and much more.

As a breath coach, observing how others breathed revealed a lot about their emotional states, their stress levels, and how they are likely to interact with and react to the world around them. This awareness not only provided an understanding of the profound impact dysfunctional breathing has on our lives, but it also showed that dysfunctional breathing can lead to increased anxiety and poorer stress management.

During times of life challenges, one of the most powerful things we can do is practise mindful, controlled breathing. As you do, you will directly mitigate the side effects of this phase, enhancing your ability to remain present, calm, and effective in your daily interactions and overall life challenges.

The 21-day energy transformation practice in 'Inner Power Game' helps you integrate breath-work into your daily routine, as a form of internal exercise that is as crucial as the food you eat or for the sleep you strive to improve. It is a practice that nurtures not only the body but also the soul, fostering a deep, harmonious connection between your inner and outer worlds.

This connection is essential for emotional healing and spiritual growth, as it aligns your physical state with your spiritual aspirations, leading to a more balanced, healthy, and fulfilled life.

The most common feedback from students who have undertaken the 21 day energy practices is that the breath practices help them to not only energise their whole being ready for the day, but also help them sleep better. You can experience this breath-work practice in day one of the programme free here:

Big Energy via Meditation & Shamanic Journeying: Reconnecting to Your Inner Child

Incorporating inner child work into meditation and shamanic practices can profoundly accelerate the healing process, especially during awakening phases. These tools, when combined, act as a gateway to reconnecting with your authentic self, and are a vital step in embodying your Big Energy and stepping fully into your purpose.

One of the frequent questions I get asked is: "what is the difference between meditation and shamanic journeying?" Let me clarify for you the way I see it.

Meditation is a practice of quieting the mind and creating a space for stillness and presence. It involves focusing your attention inward, often through breathwork or guided visualisation, allowing you to access a calm and centred state.

This peaceful state provides a safe environment for introspection, where the subconscious mind can gently reveal deeper layers of your being. It is in this mental sanctuary that your inner child can come forward, ready to be nurtured and healed.

Shamanic journeying takes meditation a step further. It is a spiritual practice rooted in ancient traditions, where the individual enters a trance-like state to explore non-ordinary realities. Guided by rhythm, such as drumming or other repetitive sounds, you can traverse symbolic landscapes of the subconscious.

These realms are rich with meaning, offering profound opportunities to meet and interact with parts of yourself that are often inaccessible in daily life, such as your inner child. In this sacred space, emotional wounds can be healed, wisdom can be uncovered, and personal transformation can occur.

Another question I get asked is: 'What is the inner child?' A term thrown about so often it can often feel like a gimmick.

The inner child stands for a vital part of your subconscious that holds memories, emotions, and experiences from your formative years. This aspect of you carries not only the joy, curiosity, and innocence of childhood but also the wounds and traumas that may have been buried over time. The inner child retains unprocessed pain, unresolved emotions, and forgotten experiences that continue to influence your behaviour, relationships, and emotional health as an adult.

Healing the inner child is essential because this younger part of you is often the key to unlocking the blocks that prevent you from fully stepping into your purpose and potential. By addressing and nurturing this part of yourself, you release old patterns, fears, and anxieties that no longer serve you, creating space for growth and transformation.

However, one of the most common challenges I've observed is that many practitioners approach inner child healing in a purely logical or task-oriented way. Clients are often given prescriptive actions like journaling prompts, affirmations, or exercises to 'fix' their inner child. While these can be helpful in some cases, they are often temporary solutions that fail to address the root cause of the issue.

I've worked with clients who have found these approaches overwhelming, especially amidst the busyness of their lives. They struggle to keep up with the tasks or feel disconnected from the process, leading to frustration or a sense of failure. The truth is, inner child work that relies solely on logic misses a crucial point: the wounds of the inner child are not logical, they are deeply emotional and energetic.

This is why I advocate for an energetic approach to inner child healing. Unlike task-driven methods, working energetically requires less conscious 'effort' because it bypasses the thinking mind and works directly with the subconscious and the soul. Instead of trying to 'fix' the inner child, you create a space where healing happens naturally, from the root.

Meditation and shamanic journeying are profound tools for exploring the depths of your consciousness and reconnecting with your inner child in ways that feel intuitive and deeply transformative.

Through meditation, you quiet the mind and create a safe, tranquil space for your inner child to emerge. In this stillness, you can meet this younger part of yourself with compassion, listen to its needs, and begin the process of healing without forcing or analysing. It is not about 'doing' something, it is about *being* present, allowing the inner child to feel seen, heard, and held.

Shamanic journeying takes this work even deeper, guiding you into symbolic realms where you can interact with your inner child on an energetic level. In these journeys, you may find yourself in a lush forest, a comforting home, or standing before a symbolic object that represents your inner child. The experiences are vivid and intuitive, offering insights and healing that transcend the ordinary.

This approach works because it speaks the language of the subconscious. Where logical methods often focus on the mind, energetic approaches like meditation and shamanic journeying work with the emotional and spiritual layers of your being. They address the root of the wounds, not just the symptoms, allowing for lasting transformation.

When inner child healing is approached energetically, it becomes less about doing and more about allowing. It is a gentle, intuitive process that does not require constant effort or perfection. Instead, it invites you to simply show up and be present with yourself. This is why it works so well, even for clients who feel overwhelmed or disconnected.

The beauty of this approach is that it integrates the healing into your entire being, creating shifts that ripple through every aspect of your life. It is not just about healing old wounds; it's about empowering your inner child to step into joy, creativity, and freedom, and allowing those qualities to flow into your present-day self.

By letting go of the need to 'fix' and embracing the energy of transformation, you unlock a path to deeper healing and connection. The result? A life that feels more aligned with your true self, where you can embody your Big Energy with ease and grace.

In my own journey, and through my work with women navigating transformative phases in their lives, I have witnessed how these practices accelerate healing. They provide a space to reconnect with the lost parts of us and address the root causes of deep-seated fears and anxieties. The inner child, once acknowledged and nurtured, becomes a powerful ally in helping us reclaim our joy, innocence, and curiosity, qualities that often get buried under the weight of adult responsibilities.

When I first began incorporating inner child work into my spiritual practices, I realised how much of my past was still shaping my present. I remember a particular shamanic journey where I found myself in a vast, open meadow. In the centre of this meadow, I saw a small version of myself, perhaps five or six years old, sitting alone, looking scared and unsure.

Through the imagery of the journey, I approached her gently and knelt beside her. I asked what she needed. Her answer, although not verbal, came through as a wave of emotion: *She needed to feel safe and not to be abandoned.* In that moment I embraced her, promising to protect her, to listen to her, and to create a life where she would feel loved and secure.

That experience shifted something profound within me. I began to understand how much of my fear and hesitation as an adult was rooted in that small, scared child within me. By reconnecting with her, I could finally begin to release those old patterns and step into a version of myself that felt freer and more empowered.

Because after this session, a memory of a six or seven-year old me, not being picked up after school came to the surface. Where a teacher had to take me to her home and I remember the fear that I felt that no-one would ever come for me. I wasn't even conscious that this memory was holding me back.

Inner child work within meditation and shamanic journeying is transformative because it does not just address surface-level issues, it goes straight to the core. It allows you to rewrite the stories you have unconsciously carried and to nurture the parts of yourself that have been longing for attention.

Many of my clients have experienced breakthroughs through these practices, often within a brief period of time. They have described the process as a return to themselves, a shedding of old baggage and a rekindling of the joy and openness they thought was lost forever.

This is not just healing; it is transformation. When you reconnect with your inner child, you reclaim the energy, wonder, and fearlessness that were always yours. You empower yourself to live a life aligned with your true spirit and purpose.

An Invitation to You

The journey to heal and reconnect with your inner child is both magical and challenging. It requires patience and compassion, but the rewards - freedom, peace, and a deeper connection to your authentic - self are immeasurable.

So, I invite you to begin this work. Whether it is through meditation, shamanic journeying, or simply taking quiet moments to listen within, give your inner child the attention and love they have been waiting for. This journey is a vital part of stepping into your Big Energy and living a life that feels truly aligned with who you are.

Your inner child is waiting for you. Are you ready to listen?

I invite you to an inner child meditation where I will guide you through a journey with your inner child. You can experience an 'Inner Child Healing Meditation in the 21-day Energy Transformation' here:

Big Energy
via Spirit Animals

Who would have thought working with 'animals' and stepping into your power and Big Energy goes together? But they do!

Working with spirit animals is an enriching practice deeply rooted in various Indigenous cultures and shamanic traditions around the world. In my experience, spirit animals often emerge during moments of spiritual awakening as guides, protectors, and mentors, helping individuals navigate the complexities of their spiritual journey.

The concept of spirit animals is grounded in the belief that each person has one or more spirit guides in the form of animals, whose traits provide insight, strength, and guidance relevant to their life path. These animals embody symbolic characteristics that resonate with the individual's current challenges or aspirations.

Spirit animals can appear during pivotal moments of transformation, offering comfort, wisdom, and a deeper connection to both the earthly and spiritual realms. They play an instrumental role in healing by illuminating areas of vulnerability and strength, while enhancing an understanding of personal power and the interconnectedness of all life. Engaging with spirit animals can lead to profound self-discovery, helping to overcome obstacles, revealing innate abilities, and aligning us more closely with our true selves.

This practice is documented across various cultures, including Native American, Celtic, and Aboriginal traditions, showcasing a universal respect for nature and its creatures as integral to human spiritual welfare. Embracing the presence of a spirit animal allows you to tap into powerful symbols of the psyche, unlocking layers of meaning and insight that propel personal and spiritual growth.

Years ago, during a meditation session at my London Victorian flat, where the hallway held a unique vibration, I experienced a vision that marked the beginning of my 10-year awakening journey. I remember an earlier tenant telling me she had seen a ghost in the hallway. Although the idea never scared me, it reinforced the notion that the house was energetically significant, a sentiment felt by anyone sensitive to such energies.

During that meditation, I had the clearest vision: a miniature human riding an eagle as it took flight from what seemed to be a cliff. The eagle, leading a group of other eagles, soared with an energy that resonated deeply within me.

This was back in 2013, at the start of my spiritual awakening. I have since noticed that birds appearing in meditations or dreams always seem to foretell momentous events in my life.

This connection extends beyond meditative or dream states into real-life experiences. At the age of 14, I vividly recall seeing a colourful bird outside my boarding school's fence. At the time, I longed to see my father, whom I had not seen in months. Instinctively, I spoke to the bird, asking it to carry a message to my father, telling him I missed him. The bird flew away, and I did not think much of it.

A few days later, I was unexpectedly called to the headmistress's office. Convinced I was in trouble, I walked in only to find my father waiting for me. He had travelled hours to see me on a non-visiting day, something he had never done before or since. It was the only time I ever saw him at my school.

Over the years, I have learnt to pay attention to birds that appear significant in my meditations, dreams, and real life. Recently, when I bought my current home, I felt apprehensive and asked for a sign. As I drove to view the house and its surroundings, a crow or raven flew ahead of me, in line with my car. When I arrived at the house, I noticed, for the first time, a tree behind it where the bird was perched. Its presence felt guiding, as if giving me a positive sign. I have learnt to discern and interpret these moments as messages from my spirit animal guides.

How to Connect with Your Spirit Animal Guides

Connecting with your spirit animal guides can be a transformative practice. Here are some ways to build that connection:

1. Meditation: Create a quiet space where you can be still and invite your spirit animal to reveal itself. Focus on your breath and remain open to any images, feelings, or symbols that come to mind.

2. Dream Journaling: Keep a journal by your bed and write down any dreams involving animals. Reflect on these dreams to uncover their significance and what they might be trying to tell you.

3. Nature Walks: Spend time in nature, observing the wildlife around you. Pay attention to any animals that appear repeatedly or seem to draw your attention.

4. Visualisation: Picture yourself in a serene environment, such as a forest or open field, and call upon your spirit animal. Notice any animal that approaches or interacts with you in this mental space.

5. Ask for Signs: Simply ask your spirit animal to show itself to you in a way that you will recognise. Be patient and mindful of any encounters, even subtle ones, which may follow.

By cultivating these practices, you invite the presence of your spirit animal into your life and strengthen the connection to your inner guidance and spiritual path.

I give guided meditation practices on journeying with your spirit animal in the 21-day Energy Transformation Programme.

Big Energy via Your Own Higher Self - The Soul Self

I once had an experience which I termed 'a conversation with the soul.' This started during episodes when I began to see vivid images in dreams, encounter spiritual beings, and channel messages that I could not, in a million years, have invented.

On the 29th of December 2016, I remember having a precise vision during a meditation session focused on Ajna (third eye), which I wrote in my journal:

∽

Today I awakened my ancient soul.

I went asking, 'what is my purpose, what is my mission here?'

I found myself walking in the woods, barefoot on golden leaves, approaching a mountain-like cave.

At the foot of the cave stands an entity I do not see clearly… a woman, perhaps? The entrance to the cave is open, and it takes me a while to enter (hesitation). Inside, it is dark and expansive.

I instinctively started a mantra:
'Awaken, child, what is your mission?
Awaken, child, what is your mission?

Awaken, child, what is your mission?' I repeated this over and over again.

Inside the cave, I see a girl-like figure in the darkest part of the space. She sits up, and I take her hand to help her stand.

In the middle of the cave, there is an opening with light streaming from above, illuminating a feminine entity wrapped entirely in white. At first glance, she appears like a waterfall. I do not see a face, but as I attempt to communicate, she shape shifts… alien-like to human-like, and then to a woman wrapped in white from head to toe.

Using my usual mantras, I say things like, 'I am love,' and 'I am God's presence' (perhaps out of fear).

She told me (not verbally), or I came to understand: 'This has no meaning here. You cannot use the way of the world here.'

I noticed again how dark and wet the cave was, and I thought… 'If I am from here, am I good or bad?' I asked, 'Are we good or bad?'

She said: 'We are neither. We just ARE.'

There was no direct answer to my question about my mission on earth, but I knew I had found a place I needed to return to, a space where I would learn how to ask the right questions.

I asked if I would find this place again, and I felt, with certainty, that I would.

As I left the cave, I emerged as a butterfly, flying out.

This was a vision I had already glimpsed even before we left the cave, while I was conversing with the entity.

◦◦◦

You see, putting on your Big Energy is your transformation - the metamorphosis process and the emergence of your butterfly.

The soul self is the deepest, most untainted part of who we are. It is the eternal essence, untouched by time and the limitations of our human experience. This aspect of us is ever-present, watching, guiding, and waiting for us to acknowledge it.

It is where our Big Energy originates, the boundless source that fuels our growth, intuition, and purpose.

When we connect with our soul self, we tap into an infinite well of wisdom and power. This connection transcends the mind's limitations and moves beyond the surface of everyday life. It invites us to listen with more than just our ears and to see with more than just our eyes. The soul-self embodies an energy that is unbound by fear or the constructs of right or wrong. It simply **is** pure consciousness, alive and expansive.

Understanding and embracing the soul-self means recognising that our worth and our power are not defined by external measures but by the richness of our inner world. It is through this connection that we find the courage to transform, to break free from self-imposed boundaries, and to step fully into our #Big Energy.

This is the energy that allows us to experience life not just as a series of challenges but as a journey of growth, expression, and continuous evolution.

Putting on your Big Energy pants, then, is more than just a moment of courage. It is a commitment to honour the voice of the soul, to trust the unseen, and to walk through life knowing that we are not just surviving but consciously becoming. It is in this becoming that the metamorphosis happens, and we take flight, embodying the true essence of our being.

Big Energy via the Spirit Guides

Spirit guides, like spirit animals, are essential companions on the journey of self-discovery and healing. They provide counsel, insight, and support, helping us navigate challenges and tap into our highest potential. While the idea of spirit guides may seem abstract to some, my own journey and those of the women I have worked with, has revealed their presence in unmistakable ways.

One of the most profound ways I experienced the power of spirit guides was during a phase of my life that I introduced earlier: the diagnosis of my brain tumour. In the introduction, I shared how this diagnosis became the catalyst for profound transformation, culminating in a dream where a spiritual being removed a lump from my head.

What I did not elaborate on was how this experience deepened my connection to spirit guides and altered my understanding of the spiritual journey.

After that dream and the subsequent confirmation of my healing, I began to reflect on the sequence of events leading up to that moment. The dream itself felt like a pivotal message, but I realised it was part of a larger pattern. There had been subtle signs, synchronicities, and intuitive nudges along the way, all of which pointed to the guidance I was receiving from the unseen realm.

How Spirit Guides Shape Our Journey

Spirit guides are not just entities that appear in moments of crisis; they are ever-present, working behind the scenes to support, guide, and protect us. For me, the tumour was not just a medical condition; it was a wake-up call. It forced me to pause, look inward, and reconnect with parts of myself that had been dormant. The dream was simply the culmination of a process that had been unfolding all along.

The guides helped me in ways I could not fully understand at the time. They provided clarity when I was overwhelmed, comfort when I felt helpless, and a sense of purpose that gave me the strength to move forward. Their guidance did not just lead to physical healing; it reignited my spiritual awareness and my connection to the energy that flows within and around us all.

This experience taught me that spirit guides are deeply intertwined with our Big Energy. They remind us of our spiritual essence, the part of us that transcends fear, doubt, and limitation. When we open ourselves to their presence, we tap into a wellspring of wisdom, strength, and love that can guide us through even the darkest moments.

Your connection to your spirit guides might not involve a life-changing dream or a miraculous healing. It could be as simple as a quiet feeling of reassurance in a difficult moment, a sign that shows up when you need it most, or an intuitive nudge that helps you make a pivotal decision.

But the truth is, they are always there. The question is, are you listening?

Encounters with the Giants

My connection to spirit guides continued to deepen after this experience. One recurring presence in my dreams was what I came to call 'the giants.'

I wrote about one such encounter in my journal:

The giants came again. Two of them. It seemed everyone was expecting them. People lined up to see them. I was not planning to stay, but for some reason, I did. I did not see them land, but I knew they were there. They spoke to me. They told me to do something simple, but when I woke up, I could not remember what.

These dreams of the giants became a recurring theme, and their guidance often came before pivotal moments in my life.

One of the most unsettling instances occurred before I went on a retreat in Greece. In a dream, I found myself in a dark place filled with women who were being held captive, victims of trafficking. Their lips were sealed shut, as though by invisible threads, and they were being watched over by men.

When I realised what kind of place I was in, I tried to escape, but all the windows and doors were locked. I remember looking out of one window and seeing people going about their mundane lives. I saw rush hour traffic, and people heading to work. They felt so close, yet I could not reach them for help.

In the corridor, I saw the giants again. I begged them for help. They did not speak, but I followed them down the corridor and I woke up.

At the time, I thought it was just a strange dream. But weeks later, when I arrived at an international all-women retreat that I had booked, I recognised the place at once . It was the exact setting from my dream, bar a few nuances in decorations. The energy was uncomfortable at times, and because of the forewarning in my dream, I was able to act consciously. I left the retreat early, trusting my intuition and the guidance I had received.

These experiences, while deeply personal, are a testament to the profound role spirit guides can play in our lives. They help us navigate challenges, illuminate the path forward, and connect us to the divine.

In my case, the guidance I received was not just about physical healing; it was about stepping into a higher version of myself, one that could trust the unseen and embrace the unknown.

Whether they appear in dreams, through meditation, or in quiet moments of clarity, spirit guides are here to remind us that we are never alone. They invite us to trust in the magic of the universe and to recognise that we are part of something far greater than we can imagine.

So, I leave you with this thought: What if the guidance you seek is already within reach? What if the answers you long for are waiting to reveal themselves, if only you allow yourself to listen?

The story of my healing is just one example of how spirit guides work with us to facilitate growth, healing, and transformation. They remind us that we are never alone, even when life feels overwhelming.

As you move through this book, I encourage you to open yourself to their presence. Begin to notice the signs and synchronicities in your own life. Trust your intuition and remember that the guidance you seek is already within you, waiting to be heard. And as you align with your inner guidance, you will unlock a whole new level of Big Energy, one that can transform not just your challenges but your entire way of being.

✱

A Simple Evocation to Call upon and Journey with Your Own Guides with Meditation

Before you enter your meditation, recite this:

'I wish to seek counsel for safe passage.

I ask for guidance on my next step in (Say what you want guidance on).

I ask for help with stepping into flow, alignment, health, love and expansion as I step into it.

Feel into what you are calling in.

Close your eyes and allow your third eye to take you on a journey.

Do not force anything and allow all visualisations as they drop. Some visions may not make sense and feel random. It is also easy to get excited about your download, however, so stay grounded and just allow it all without emotional attachment.

*

Big Energy via the Power of Your Dream State

As I've analysed my dreams over the years, I've come to realise that dreams are more than just fleeting images of the subconscious mind. They are profound reflections of our inner world, fragments of subconscious processing, echoes of past life experiences, and even foretellings of what is yet to come.

For me, my dreams have always been a combination of these three.

Some dreams arrive as warnings or premonitions, foretelling events in my life. Yet, interestingly, I've noticed that real-life events don't always unfold to the extreme that the dreams do. Often, things stop short, like a movie suddenly pausing before reaching its climax. It makes me wonder: what if these dreams represent a cycle I have lived before? And what if, in this lifetime, I am more aware, more grounded, and I am breaking karmic patterns before they fully play out?

Karma is often misunderstood as a simple system of punishment and reward; 'you do bad, bad things happen; you do good, good things happen.' But in truth, karma is much deeper than that. It is the unseen thread weaving together our actions, thoughts, and choices across time. It is the energy we create and the lessons we must learn.

From a spiritual perspective, karma is the soul's way of evolving. It is a cycle of cause and effect, guiding us toward healing, awareness, and ultimately, freedom. Some believe that our dreams can reveal unresolved karma i.e. patterns we have lived through before, but which we now have the opportunity to transform.

So when I wake from a dream that seems all too real, when I experience a vision that feels like déjà vu, I often ask myself: am I being shown a past cycle? Am I meant to break this pattern before it repeats?

Regardless, I have come to see my dreams as a map, a guide through my life's journey.

And this is why dream work is such a powerful Big Energy tool.

One of the best ways to understand your dreams is to document them. Writing down your dreams helps you develop a deeper awareness of their messages.

Some dreams come once and leave a strong imprint, while others return over and over, revealing hidden patterns or marking different seasons of life. These recurring dreams are often keys to understanding where we are on our spiritual path.

The more you write your dreams down, the more you will start to remember them. The more you remember them, the more you will begin to decode them.

The First Dream I Ever Wrote Down

I started journaling my dreams in October 2013/14, the very beginning of this book's ten-year journey. Before that, my dreams had always been significant, but I couldn't seem to retain them upon waking. My very first dream entry was simple but striking:

> Man with slight facial hair. My feet were sore; I sat down, deeply engrossed in conversation. Our faces were close together, staring straight into his face. 'You are so good looking.' Talking about 'Tantra,' showing him something on the wall, laughing, very intense, very real, very joyful.

At the time, I wrote them down with no expectation of meaning. I simply wanted to remember. But as the years passed, I saw patterns emerging.

Dreams that foretold the future - some of my dreams weren't just subconscious reflections; they were forewarnings of what was to come.

One of the first dreams that truly impacted me occurred when I was around 12 years old.

In the dream, I had died and gone to heaven. I remember being in a white, cloud-like space, not white as in colour, but white as in vastness. It was an open, expansive place where I stood with others, waiting.

Suddenly, someone called out:

'They've left the gates open!'

People began rushing toward the gates, trying to escape back to their lives. I stood frozen, unsure. Should I stay or run? Then a thought came: I need to seek advice from my mother. She will know what to do.

In an instant, I was back on earth, standing in my grandmother's living room. The women in the room sat in mourning. I realised they were grieving me. I searched for my mother and found her curled up in a chair. I tried to get her attention:

'Mummy, I need your advice.'

But she did not get up. She did not look at me. She only whispered, 'I am too weak.'

Then I woke up.

I told my grandmother about the dream, and she reassured me that dreaming of death was nothing to fear. But my mother being weak… that might be something to be concerned about.

Some months later, my mother fell gravely ill. She was passed from doctor to doctor, yet no one could determine what was wrong - a story for another time.

A similar thing happened in my senior year of secondary school. I dreamt about our PE teacher, a woman so stern and intimidating that most of us tried to avoid her. In the dream she was walking on stones, when suddenly she collapsed, arching over in pain.

That morning, I told my friend about the dream. She insisted we tell the PE teacher. After much hesitation, we made our way to her house. When we arrived, we were told she had just been rushed to the hospital. She had been pregnant, and there were complications.

Of course, my dream and this woman's predicament may have just been a coincidence; however, after this incident, I began to see my dreams as a burden. Perhaps I was meant to tell the teacher about my dream sooner, and perhaps that might have prevented something.

Fast forward to my phase of awakening, which I will discuss in more detail in the next chapters; my dreams came back in full force. Over the years, I have honed my ability to decode them.

There are dreams of spiders or insects, which always signal challenging times ahead, and dreams of snakes when big life transformations are about to begin. And then there were the dreams with animals, such as the snowy white owl or the walking trees.

Then there are the astral projections.

As I deepened my spiritual journey, my dreams expanded beyond simple visions. I began experiencing out-of-body experiences (OBEs), moments where my consciousness separated from my physical body, allowing me to witness reality from a different plane.

OBEs can occur spontaneously, during sleep, meditation, or even near-death experiences, and are often associated with a state called **astral projection** when it happens deliberately; something that became key in my spiritual work.

The first time this happened, I had just returned from a spiritual retreat in Bali. I took a nap in the afternoon, and as I woke, I realised my body wasn't moving. I was conscious, but I couldn't wake up physically.

Suddenly, I was floating around my house, observing it from above. I felt a moment of panic. What if my body is found here while I am away from it?! Then I decided to return to my body which was lying on the couch where I had taken a nap.

A few years later, a similar experience happened. I woke up and tried to reach for my phone, but my hand went through the phone not able to physically grab it. Again, I experienced myself venturing round my home, leaving my physical body behind. Everything seems so vivid, but some details are not the same. For example, the house felt super clean, luxurious and I could see water, as if I lived near a river or the sea. I eventually made it back to my bed upstairs, and when I woke physically the phone was exactly where I had been trying to grab it.

Each time I experienced astral projection, I felt a deep sense of renewal. And every time, things in my world started to move at an accelerated pace.

Over the years, dreams have become a tool for foretelling events in my life, and they can be the same for you and consequently one of your Big Energy abilities.

Going Forward

Dreams are powerful portals into our subconscious mind, spiritual guidance, and even our past and future.

If you want to begin working with your dreams, start with these steps:

Write them down immediately upon waking. Your memory fades quickly, and the more you practice writing them down, the more you'll remember over time.

Pay attention to how you feel in the dream. The emotions in the dream often hold more meaning than the imagery itself.

Notice recurring themes. Certain symbols and experiences tend to repeat during specific seasons of life, offering messages about where you are on your journey.

Trust the process. Don't over analyse; allow the messages to unfold naturally.

Dreams are one of the most accessible ways to tap into your Big Energy. By honouring them, you are honouring the deepest wisdom within yourself.

And as we move into the next chapter, we will explore even more ways to harness these insights and step fully into your power.

CHAPTER 4:

Path to Exponential Growth

Here we focus on the importance of letting go of past traumas, limiting beliefs, and negative patterns that can obstruct spiritual growth. Now we have our Big Energy pants tools and know how to use them; in order to better utilise the spiritual awakening phase, we must ensure we are clearing what needs to be cleared. As we do so, we are making a path for growth and a more conscious way of creating our own lives.

Whenever our soul is ready for our human to evolve into the new (such as a new level of reality), it is also a time of shedding what no longer serves us in preparation to bring in the things that our soul desires, our next level evolution.

This process can feel uncomfortable, scary, and even painful at times.

On a practical and physical level, shedding the old skin can manifest as releasing: a loved one, a relationship that no longer works, a job, a possession, an old pattern, outdated limiting belief, etc.

Whatever it is for you, will come to the surface as an experience to navigate.

It is very normal to try to hold on to these things which, as a result, can bring about anxiety, struggle or even feeling blocked on your exponential growth journey.

We are agents of change.

We are meant to evolve, and we can only evolve through change.

Keeping it 'safe and mundane' feels comfortable, but it is not always for your highest good.

Every awakening or growth phase is an opportunity to release and heal cycles you've perhaps repeated. You deserve so much better and there is a new beginning waiting for you at the end of your comfort zone.

The following is the journey path that we use in 'Inner Power Game' as women embark on this journey of stepping into their next level, in a way that is sustainable and a framework you can easily follow as a self-practice.

Using the 'Three Journey Path to Exponential Growth' you will begin the journey of letting go of what no longer serves you and in the process make room for new opportunities and insights.

This has been the foundational journey template for every woman I have worked with, and who is now not only thriving but flourishing and showing up in the world with power and impact.

Phase 1: HEAL IT

Understanding the Obstacles
and Releasing the Wound

Our journey is often hindered by the invisible burdens we carry. Old wounds, outdated convictions, and habitual reactions that no longer serve us. These are not just mere annoyances; they form a significant barrier to our spiritual and personal development.

The first step in clearing the path is identifying and understanding the specific challenges that hold us back. These can include emotional wounds, deeply ingrained beliefs, or repetitive behaviours that create cycles of negativity. By recognising these barriers, we can begin to approach them with intention and clarity and as we do, we consciously release.

One of the biggest realisations in my own process is that releasing trauma is not about forgetting painful events but understanding and reprocessing them from a place of safety and support.

This phase focuses on using practical tools as discussed in Chapter 3 such as meditation and breath-work. These are invaluable tools that can help us work through and release these deep-seated pains, emerging into a place where we can reflect on them and see those experiences for what they truly are.

Phase 2: TRANSFORM IT

Dismantling and Transmuting Limiting Beliefs and Negative Patterns into Empowerment

Limiting beliefs are often subconscious, formed through past experiences and societal conditioning. They can dictate our behaviour and restrict our potential. Identifying these beliefs is crucial, as is understanding their origins and their impact on our lives.

Where we are not consciously transmuting the experiences presented in the obstacles, trauma and chaotic phase, it is likely that we are throwing away opportunities that were presented for our evolution.

Techniques such as those introduced in the 'Inner Power Game 21-day Energy Transformation' such as affirmations, mantra cards and journaling, can be effective in challenging and rewriting these narratives. By replacing limiting beliefs with empowering ones, we open ourselves to a broader range of possibilities and a deeper understanding of our capabilities.

Negative patterns, whether behavioural or thought-based, can become cyclical and self-perpetuating, trapping us in unfulfilling loops. Mindfulness and mindful awareness practices are powerful in recognising these patterns as they emerge.

Once aware, we can actively choose to respond differently, breaking the cycle and setting new, healthier patterns in motion and stepping into a newer version of ourselves and reality.

Phase 3: CREATE NEW
Creating Space for Growth and Stepping into Our Next Highest Version

Clearing the path is fundamentally about making space: emotionally, mentally, and spiritually, for new growth. As we shed old skins, we are reborn into a state of greater freedom and clarity. This not only enhances our spiritual connection but also improves our quality of life by allowing us to live more authentically and fully.

The process of clearing the path is continuous and requires patience and dedication. It is not always easy, as it involves facing what we most fear. However, the freedom gained through this cleansing process is invaluable.

It empowers us to move forward onto our next level with a lighter load and a clearer vision, ready to embrace the profound transformations that this new reality has to offer.

Often, I see where a woman is trying to up-level her life, or to follow her calling of stepping deeper and bigger into her purpose but continuously gets stuck, moves forward, but then things collapse, or she becomes overwhelmed and experiences burnout.

In the majority of cases, this is down to their energetic capacity being full of some of the energetic vibrations that could have been cleared if this process had been followed.

Real Life Scenario Exercise

Let us explore a real-life example of how to apply the three phases to overcome a common scenario of a high achieving woman who finds themselves constantly having to struggle to achieve success/desires and recognises this pattern as something they wish to change.

Phase 1: HEAL

Understanding the Pattern and Heal the Wound/Trauma Behind it

Start by reflecting on why there is a perceived need to struggle or endure hardship to demonstrate your worth or to get what you want. This often stems from early life experiences or family patterns.

For instance, if you grew up seeing a parent struggle continuously, you might subconsciously believe that true worth and success only come through hardship. When I work with clients, I see over and over again, women who have seen either one or both of their parents struggle for years. In my personal experience, I saw this in my own mum who struggled to provide and maintain stability.

In a Journaling exercise, you can begin to tweak this out gently with the following question (which can be applied to different scenarios).

- Where does this pattern stem from?
- What is your first experience of it
  (in this case - struggle)?
- Why do you feel you have to repeat
  these patterns?

If I think back, mine was in boarding school at the early age of 12/13 years old. Food supply was limited; care givers were not readily available and I had to take care of myself at such an early age. However, you could say this was already imprinted in me as I had seen my mother struggle through life.

I have a memory of us as children; my two siblings, half-brother and the three cousins staying with us at the time sitting on the floor, huddled over the same bowl of food for dinner because we had to eat in secrecy as there was not enough for the whole household, extending to the uncles (my dad's brothers) who were staying with us at that time.

Or the struggles my mother experienced after she left my dad, renting just two rooms in a house. One room was at the front of the house and the other at the back of the house. One room we used as a bedroom where my mum, my two other siblings and three cousins slept and the other room at the end of the house we kept our food provisions, clothing and kitchen utensils to cook.

From an early age, I saw my mother struggle through life. I came to believe that the process of struggle is what leads to having what we want or even that struggle always precedes what we want.

As I grew older, I came to associate struggle and discomfort with the path of growth. Which means for every up-levelling I journey through, I subconsciously manifested challenges to proceed to the next phase.

To shift this mindset, we have to rewire ourselves to believe without a doubt that this is not the case, we have to give ourselves permission and start to see proof that we do not have to go through struggles to earn our desires.

Using this process, you take the time to acknowledge the pattern you wish to clear and heal from the root, rather than filling your energetic capacity with unwanted and unresolved issues that will keep re-manifesting themselves over and over again.

Phase 2: TRANSFORM
Dismantling Limiting Beliefs
and Breaking Negative Patterns

Identify and challenge the belief that struggle is synonymous with worth. Through cognitive restructuring, a technique used in cognitive-behavioural therapy, you can actively replace this limiting belief with a more empowering one, for example using affirmations.

Affirmations are a form of declaration of what we want and desire to be. For example:

*'My worth is inherent, and I deserve to
achieve my goals with grace and ease.*

I AM ease, I am grace.'

Regularly affirming a new belief can profoundly alter
your self-view and life approach.

With this sort of affirmation, you could then silently
challenge yourself with little curiosity statements like:

'How easy can it be?'

A note of caution with affirmations. Many people use
affirmations, which is great; but affirmations do not
work if we do not really believe the words we are saying.
This is why affirmations fail for so many. You can utter
the words until kingdom come, but if you do not really
believe the affirmation with every fibre in your body, it
will not come to be.

Affirmations can be powerful – but only if we feel
strongly connected to them.

So how can you create your own affirmations in ways
that truly vibrate with your true essence?

I often work with my clients to create their
affirmations from the 'Power Boundary' work (explained
below) we do together. This way, your affirmations
themselves have a powerful energetic vibration that
clothes-you-in and expands you into different resonances.

Mindfulness is key here in breaking any cycle. Practice being present and consciously choose responses that align with your new belief in worthiness without struggle, as in the following scenario:

When faced with challenges, instead of defaulting to a struggle mindset, ask, *How can I handle this with ease?* This helps in establishing new, healthier patterns of navigating not just moments of growth but spiritual awakenings.

In this instance, I would reflect on this question:

If you no longer believed that struggle was necessary, how would you approach your goals?

For me, it was a realisation that I would totally take the steps to go for what I want (without attachments to the end goal), believing I can get it and that it can be easy. I would follow the intuitive nudges, not with fear but with excitement.

In this phase, I would double down on self-care and embodiment practices (more on this in Part Two) celebrating who I am becoming, not because of the physical manifestation but more because of how I feel with the increased frequency and vibration of all that I am to be taking these steps.

The new belief we want to create here is to envision a life where ease and worthiness coexist as this can fundamentally change our trajectory of future awakenings, bringing us exponential growth.

Phase 3: CREATE IT –
Creating Space for Growth and
Stepping into Our Next Highest Version

Implement the Inner Power Game Boundary Process to protect and reinforce your new mindset. Decide that struggle is not your default state, but ease.

A Guide to Inner Power Game Boundary Work

Power Boundaries are like the values we create for ourselves, that helps us stay firmly rooted in our power. For me, establishing power boundaries is about setting clear agreements on how I will show up in various contexts, defined by what I allow into my energy field and what I do not.

In the practice of dismantling the wound and trauma such as in this scenario for example, we could use power boundaries as the promises we make to nurture our inner child where the trauma first arose, especially when others may overlook our needs. These boundaries are not just protective shields but are active statements of self-care and self-respect.

As we clear the path of trauma and remove obstacles to make way for desired changes in our lives, power boundaries play a crucial role. They help us create space for growth by defining what we accept in our personal growth journeys and what we choose to leave behind.

Acting in alignment with these boundaries sends a strong message and sets a tone for how we allow others to treat us, how we present ourselves in various situations, and what we attract into our lives energetically. Adhering to these boundaries enables us to maintain our integrity and ensures that our interactions and personal spaces are aligned with our true selves.

Power boundaries are one of my most potent resources and practices within the 'Inner Power Game' producing tangible and exponential results. They empower us to live authentically and foster environments where we can thrive both personally and spiritually.

In the 'Inner Power Game 21-day Energy Transformation', you are guided through a process of creating these power boundaries for the life you want.

By setting boundaries around how you engage with challenges and opportunities, you affirm that your dreams and desires are attainable without undue hardship. This opens up space for growth that is free from old constraints. In this situation, it looks like this:

> *'I value myself just that little bit more and know that struggle is not my natural state and therefore I do not resort to it, to step into a next level. This way I bring forth my dreams and desires because they are part of me already.'*

As you do, you are creating space in your energetics, which is filled with new experiences based on your new expectation of what you are open or not open to. We can also say that you begin to become an energetic match for what you want, and this is why, at times, my own clients feel like things started to happen for them in ways that feel like magic!

By applying these three phases of heal, transform and create you systematically clear the path of old beliefs and patterns that no longer serve you, making way for a life defined by self-worth and ease, rather than struggle and hardship.

Dialogue with the Guides on Stagnation:

'Humanity is at a standstill, spirituality is in ascension, there is no block,' they said.

'So why am I not moving forward or am I? Am I doing everything as I should?' I asked

'You are exactly where you should be, and everything is here for you. If only you could open your eyes to it. Everything that you feel is calling to you is here to make it happen. Do more of what you feel is calling.'

'I desire to be doing more of my work, and earning in high value; with that I desire to balance both sides,' I said.

'We are not about the desires, for that means little. We are more about who you are. The desire is only part of that.'

'I ask for your help' I said - like a child lost, surrendering.

'You are more powerful than you know. We are at your service.

Step back into your power.

A simple journaling of the things that you feel are showing up in your horizon and yet not just there will suffice.'

✷

A Simple Exercise
To close this chapter, this is a good point to journal out what you are currently experiencing generally in your life. As you journal, make a silent inner conviction that as you journal you release what needs to drop.

PART TWO

TRANSFORM:
TOOLS FOR POWERFUL
TRANSFORMATION

CHAPTER 5

Self-Love, Self-Care, and Self-Worth as Tools for Transformation

Let me tell you one of the biggest things that has helped me the most, in not just transforming my life, but holding on to my Big Energy: my ability to romanticise my life, be intentional in making even the smallest thing sacred, even when things were tough!

This hasn't come easy and it is still something I work on, but at the cornerstone of it is self-love. If you have ever felt guilty of giving to yourself or celebrating your accomplishment or who you are - it's time to drop that guilt!

Here is why: opening ourselves to love and cultivating self-love, self-care, and compassion forms the basis of deep personal growth and feeling worthy to have your deepest desires.

As we navigate the path to a more enlightened self, embracing these practices is not merely beneficial, it is essential. Through self-love, we learn to honour our needs and boundaries; through self-care, we maintain our physical and emotional health; and through compassion, we extend our understanding and kindness outwards, enriching our interactions with the world.

Together, self-love, self-care, and compassion not only enhance our own lives but also empower us to contribute positively to the lives of others, creating a ripple effect of healing and transformation.

In my experience, I also found that the more I incorporate these practices, the more I am able to move from not just creating to meet basic needs but going beyond, into desires.

Self-care provides the foundation for self-love to grow, and help us feel worthy and deserving of happiness, success, and all the things that we will otherwise be afraid to dream of/not feel worthy of.

Self-love, in turn, allows us to set the boundaries to make the choices that are in our own best interest and prioritise our own wellbeing. It is also the key to helping others know how to treat us in a way that is favourable.

Both self-care and self-love should be part of an ongoing process that requires consistent effort. The problem comes from the fact that many of us neglect these two aspects, especially in moments of growth or awakenings. It is often the last thing on our agenda as we navigate our endless 'to do' lists or goals.

As we navigate life, paying less attention to this aspect, we forget what really lights us up.

The acts of self-care and self-love can be powerful

in several ways, as already mentioned. In the process of a spiritual awakening, they can become even more powerful tools, which is why it is important to double down on them.

The conscious act of self-care and self-love improves your overall wellbeing. As you take care of your physical, mental, and emotional states, this leads to an improved physical health, helps reduce stress and to step effortlessly into the state of happiness that many look for but do not know how to reach.

It also improves your self-esteem and self-worth - like in the case of my client who felt her partner was not making her happy – so she started doing this herself and taking responsibility for her own happiness. The whole dynamic changed and now she feels more worthy and has stopped waiting for someone else to give her what was already within.

The magical part of this practice is that you start to attract good things to you because like attracts like. This is a magnetic way of creating the life you want including building stronger relationships.

These simple acts of self-care and self-love help us initiate the inner fulfilment that most of us desire. The other thing to mention is around empowerment. By valuing taking care of ourselves, we break free from certain expectations and pressure that we may feel from either society or from family and friends.

Building Resilience and Energetic Capacity

Self-care and self-love practices can help you develop greater resilience, both physically and mentally, which can be beneficial when we are dealing with big life challenges and difficulties or issues that usually arise in this phase of awakening or growth. By developing this strong resilience, only then can you start to build momentum, where you are able to not only achieve bigger goals, but sustain what you already have without self-sabotage through old patterns.

When we take care of ourselves and we start to love ourselves, we are more likely to be able to achieve our goals and aspirations in life, because right here you are expanding what I like to call your 'energetic capacity.'

And it just becomes more beautiful. You start to find more balance in life because, again, self-care and self-love practices can help us find this balance between our personal and professional lives leading us to this satisfaction and fulfilment with how we are living our life overall.

Already you can see that self-love and self-care sound so simple, and something we can almost take for granted, yet they are key to keeping or activating this kind of inner power that changes everything in our life.

However, so many people are missing out and do not prioritise self-care or self-love. There is often an expectation from society, especially, when it comes to women, that women are expected to prioritise the needs of others over their own. They tend to start to feel guilty for taking time for themselves. This is one of the big reasons why I see many not using this beautiful practice that can change most of their problems.

In addition, most are often juggling so many things at the same time— multiple priorities, such as work, family, household tasks and other types of responsibilities—that they feel they cannot have time to prioritise self-care.

When I give a client homework to prioritise self-care and self-love for a period of time, the other excuse I get is money. Many have developed the mindset around self-care as a luxurious activity that can be expensive. Consequently, they make up their minds that they do not have the financial resources to invest in some of the self-care activities they feel will count. In fact, we can start small. Even just some time in the bath, a longer time in the shower, a walk, time away from the family – these all count. So, there are many things we can do that do not cost money, but automatically people start to think that self-care will be expensive.

Reasons why so few people are doing it

Until recently, there has been a lack of full representation and role models actively promoting these sorts of practices or habits in most people's private and immediate circle.

Men and women may not see the representation of self-care and self-love in their family circle, society, or workplace where the culture has seen more masculine energy dominate; where burnout, goals, achievement and physical power are the features of success.

We need more people talking about their self-care, and their self-love practice and how they prioritise it; and it all starts with each one of us. The more we make it a theme or a priority, and the more we make it a normality, we will encourage the people around us to also start to make it an important practice that is considered worthy enough.

When you start to see self-care and self-love practices as a spiritual practice (as opposed to a selfish act) that connects you to something so much bigger - your Big Energy - it enables you to show up in that frequency, and you may become intentional about it.

*

Simple Exercise:
Set aside 15 minutes of your day, to make self-care a priority.

What does this mean for you?

Perhaps being mindful of your own needs, making self-care a priority over other activities and responsibilities, saying no to things that do not serve you well or nourish you; and making time for things that do.

This means putting yourself first. And yes, I know, for so many people this is a massive thing. But if we are going to do this right, we need to make 'us' a priority. This does not mean becoming selfish and not caring about others. It just means developing a process of knowing that your happiness starts with you and what you radiate out.

Along my own transformation journey, there were clear indications of my lack of self-worth over the years. Jobs I had taken where they desperately needed someone to help them transition; so it was only ever temporary work (although this has now become a strength of mine). In relationships, meeting men in their transitioning period as they leave long-term relationships, only for them to get stronger and then leave me. Or dating men who did not meet my feminine spiritual desire for deepness and yet still giving them my all.

How was I valuing myself in all these instances? Did I not feel worthy of going for what my soul truly desired? The result is unmistakable evidence of attachment to struggle, chaos and challenging times. Because it seems this was how I justified my worth, by the ability to move through tough times. I knew that I had an immense energy that I brought to my work and my relationships and yet I did not trust that I was worthy enough. It was this moment of realisation that awakened the desire to value myself more. And this journey is one that starts with self-care and self-love. Do not wait for others to romance you – 'romanticise your whole life and everyday' is what I say!

Only when we value ourselves and feel worthy, knowing we are the ones we have been waiting for (or at least take forward moves towards it) only then are we able to fully capitalise on the potential that is available to us from our Big Energy.

Over and over, I see one of the biggest factors when people do not prioritise themselves is the fear of abandonment by others. Consequently, they lose themselves in the fight to hold on to the other.

The fear of abandonment by the masculine was one of my biggest issues to heal in my journey of fully stepping into my Big Energy. As a child growing up in Africa, I constantly heard my mother and aunties say, 'men just want sex, after sex they will leave'. And I look back at the eight-year-old me, whose own father was not present.

On my journey to healing and clearing these misalignment fragments, in one particular meditative journaling session, I acknowledged this fear of abandonment. I sat in it for a while acknowledging the pain that comes with it when it does happen.

I asked myself as I felt all the discomfort:

Does this detract from my wholeness? No!
Does this detract from inner happiness? No!

Does this detract from my completeness? No!
So, what is this fear about?

I sat with it for a long time and felt into where in my life this was influencing my actions.

Again, I asked myself, 'what is the worst that could happen in a moment of abandonment?' I felt an ache in my chest, sadness. And then it happened. I recognised that this fear of abandonment is about me and not about what the other person has done or has the ability to do (abandon me) - it's literally the fear of it happening again that I fear most. And so I kept manifesting these scenarios as part of the story and fear I held.

Feeling worthy to have and to hold your wildest dream is the life lesson for many people.

Going Forward

Building self-care, self-love, and self-worth into your life does not have to be complicated. It starts with creating a routine - a 15 to 30 minute practice daily, weekly, or even monthly. This could be as simple as taking a warm bath, journaling, going for a walk, or enjoying a quiet cup of tea. The key is to make it something you can stick to, a practice that becomes as natural as brushing your teeth or preparing for the day.

This routine is more than just an act of self-care; it is a commitment to yourself. It teaches you to approach life with self-compassion, easing the harsh inner critic many of us carry. Over time, it begins to shift the way you see yourself, helping you cultivate kindness and forgiveness toward yourself.

For many, this journey is about rediscovering self-worth, a lesson that so many of us are here to learn. It's about allowing yourself to feel worthy, not just of rest and joy, but of receiving all the abundance and love life has to offer.

I encourage you to take this beyond your personal life and incorporate self-care into your work. Over time, my clients often find that they can reimagine their work schedules in ways that feel more balanced and aligned. For some, this looks like transitioning to a four-day workweek while maintaining (or even increasing) their income. For others, it is creating a day within their work week dedicated to a more relaxed, luxurious approach; what I call a 'CEO Day.'

For me, this day is Friday. I spend it at a leisure club with stunning views of a golf course and amenities like a pool, sauna, and jacuzzi. Between moments of work, I take time to nurture myself, whether that's soaking in the warm water or simply enjoying the peaceful environment. This isn't just about indulgence; it's a way of blending work with self-care, allowing me to approach my business with clarity, creativity, and joy.

The journey to self-love, self-care, and self-worth is not a one-time event; it's a lifelong practice. It's about choosing, over and over again, to prioritise yourself, not out of selfishness, but because when you nurture yourself, you can show up more fully for everything and everyone in your life.

As you move forward, ask yourself:

- What small but powerful routines can I build into my day?
- How can I show myself kindness and compassion, even when it feels uncomfortable?
- What would it look like to truly feel worthy of rest, joy, and abundance?

This chapter is not just about adding practices to your life, it's about transforming the way you see yourself. And when you begin to show yourself the love and care you deserve, you will find that life responds in kind, bringing you closer to the person you are meant to be.

So go ahead: start today. Schedule time for yourself, create that self-care routine, and watch how this small act ripples through every area of your life. Your Big Energy is waiting.

The Guides on the Energy of Love and Compassion

'Everything should be done with love and compassion because this powers up your heart, your power centre.

The way you connect to your higher selves and spirit guides is through this channel because we operate on this resonance of the heart. So, if you want to learn to hear higher guidance from the spiritual side, learn to power up the heart first.

The resonance which the heart emits is not of time, nor distance bound, as it is connected with all that there is in the universe and beyond, because they are all made of the same.

The trees are guides and keepers of all knowledge and this too is accessible to you through a connection from the heart powered by love and compassion.

This is the resonance, through which they allow you the passage to enter the realm of knowledge.'

The Guides on Rest and Sleep State

'The body needs rest. Rest is the place you go
to retire back to your true state. When you rest
you retreat from this physical journey and give
yourself permission to go back home.

The only thing is, for some they no longer know
how to rest. When you rest, you surrender and
ask to be shown the way from your higher
guidance, for in a rest mode your physical body
is out of operation, but the inner self is still in
control and more.

It is like your internal navigation kicks in.
Rest is the period where things come into
fruition, for there is less friction in energy for
manifesting ideas and dreams into reality.

Rest is your creative time. It is how your
physical self-manifested into this reality.
Rest is all you are, and it is worth remembering
how important it is.

And so, we come to the sleep state.

The sleep state is the closest you have to your
natural state. During the sleep state you are at rest

from the mind, deep into your subconscious itself. It is in this state that many of your subconscious thoughts and beliefs are revealed to you.

If you want to know what is keeping you blocked or what your perception of the physical state is like, pay attention to what happens in your sleep state. This state is also the most powerful way to manifest the life you desire, because here you are at rest. For if you can bring it in and see it clearly in the sleep/rest state, the physical state will reflect it back to you.

The sleep state is a place of manifesting because it is our true state. In this state, there is no veil between any of the worlds or beings across different dimensions. Learn to become an 'active' being in this state and you turn the mirror around for the true image.

To become awake and active in the rest state, practice activities such as meditation, visualisation, and lucid dreaming. These are all activities that allow you to become an active participant on this level.'

The Guides on Love

'Humans are afraid of love because they are afraid of their potential. The physical body is limited in its physical form, compared to its soul-self, so it is normal for the physical to resist at times. So many times, it resists total surrender to this energy of love, with the fear of losing itself to it, and losing control. Because then the soul takes over.

There is constantly a battle within, between the soul and the physical self, which is run by the ego.

The ego never wishes to lose control to the soul self, which is the God aspect of us.

You can imagine any conflict with, and breaking off from, this energy of love would be perceived as painful.

Hence a journey to let the ego aspects of ourselves, in the pursuit of love or finding God, helps us further this journey.

One cannot truly reconnect to love with the ego at play. Whilst the ego has its uses on your human journey, it often needs to be quietened to totally surrender to love and recharge your life force.'

Chapter 6

Transforming Fear, Doubt, and Impostor Syndrome

What keeps you up at night?

For many, it is the relentless whispers of self-doubt, the gnawing fear of the unknown, or the looming weight of not feeling 'enough.' These feelings are amplified in a world where bad news is a constant backdrop, where social media serves as a stage for comparison, and where success is often measured by metrics that feel far removed from our inner truth.

But here is the truth: fear, doubt, and impostor syndrome are not flaws or weaknesses. They are part of the human experience. They exist because we care about our work, our relationships, and the impact we want to make. The key is not to seek to eliminate these feelings but to transform how we relate to them, and keep in check that they are not turning into a control freak, or on the other spectrum keeping us stuck and stagnant.

Numerous times, clients have asked me how to manage the fear that creeps up out of nowhere, worry about their children, work, and, at other times, trivial things. And it feels like the mind runs wild with every potential possibility.

This is where your Big Energy comes in. Big Energy is not about suppressing fear or pretending doubt does not exist. It is about stepping into your power despite them. It is the quiet but fierce belief that who you are at your core is enough and that even in uncertainty, you have the ability and the energetic capacity to thrive.

Fear has always been a part of human life, but in today's world, it feels inescapable. Every day, we are bombarded with stories of crises, disasters, and conflicts. The media thrives on fear, knowing it keeps us engaged; but at what cost? Constant exposure to negativity leaves us feeling anxious, powerless, and disconnected from our inner calm.

And then there is the constant scrolling through curated snapshots of others' lives, which can lead to feelings of inadequacy. We see success stories and wonder, 'Why not me?' or 'What am I doing wrong?' Or even 'How do I copy that?' And then there is the information overload. Advice, opinions, and conflicting narratives filling every corner of the internet. Instead of clarity, we are left with analysis paralysis, doubting our ability to make the 'right' choice.

This relentless input does not just affect our mental state, it affects our energy. Fear, doubt, and impostor syndrome keeps us isolated from the Big Energy, leaving us stuck in cycles of inaction, overcompensation or repeating cycles and patterns that do not serve us well. To move through these challenges, it helps to understand fear, doubt, and impostor syndrome.

Fear is often rooted in the unknown. It is your mind's way of protecting you from perceived threats, even when those threats are not real.

Doubt questions your abilities and decisions, often arising from past experiences or societal conditioning.

Impostor Syndrome whispers that you are a fraud, that you do not deserve your success, or that you are not as capable as others believe you to be.

These feelings do not exist to sabotage you; they exist to protect you. But when left unchecked, they can hold you back from stepping into your full potential. Fear, doubt, and impostor syndrome do not look the same for everyone. How you experience them often depends on your personality.

For Introverts: You may internalise fear and doubt, analysing every outcome until you feel paralysed. In addition, perfectionism can keep you from taking risks, as you focus on avoiding failure rather than embracing growth.

For Extroverts: You may mask your fear with outward confidence, taking on more than you can handle to prove your worth. The constant need for external validation can leave you feeling disconnected from your inner self.

Neither response is 'wrong' but both can lead to burnout and disconnection from your Big Energy. Your Big Energy is your inner wisdom and strength; it is what connects you to something greater than yourself. It does not totally eliminate fear, doubt, or impostor syndrome, but it allows you to navigate them with grace and take back power in realising that these are not factual or real. As you take back control, when these feelings show up, you will have a better perspective on things.

Tools to Transform Fear, Doubt, and Impostor Syndrome

1. Stop the Noise

Fear thrives in chaos. Take control of what you allow into your mind and energy:

Limit exposure to the news and social media, especially before bed. Replace negative inputs with uplifting books, music, or podcasts. Practice meditation – personally for me this has been my number one tool for taking back control from particular the fear of the unknown. In my experience, meditation helps you to understand how your mind works and in so doing, you are better able to master it and to identify the patterns of your thoughts.

2. Shift Your Perspective

Fear and doubt often arise from focusing on what you lack or what could go wrong. Instead, try reframing: ask empowering questions, such as 'What's the best that could happen?' *Focus on gratitude*: for example, every morning or before bed, you could make a mental note of three things you are grateful for each day.

3. Embrace Stillness

In moments of overwhelm, pause. Whether through meditation, deep breathing, or simply sitting in silence, stillness allows you to reconnect with your Big Energy. If you find stillness difficult, like some of my clients, try something different, such as go for a walk in nature, observe a flowing river, or use visualisations tools. I create bespoke visualisation meditations that combine symbols and sounds created for a specific block for my clients (especially those that struggle with silent meditation at first), and these work wonders!

4. Work with Your Energy Type

Introverts: Focus on small, consistent actions that build confidence over time. Use journaling as a way to process fears and doubts.

Extroverts: Lean on trusted friends or mentors to share what you are feeling. Balance your outward energy with moments of solitude to recharge.

Fear is not your enemy, it is a signal. It highlights where you need to grow, where you need to trust yourself more, and where you need to let go of control. For example, a client once told me she was terrified of leaving her corporate job to start her own business. When we explored her fear, we realised it was rooted in a desire for stability and security. By acknowledging this, she was able to create a plan that honoured her need for stability while still moving toward her dream. Fear can be the nudge you need to step into your Big Energy, but only if you are willing to listen, and learn from it.

The world will always be filled with noise: bad news, opinions, and expectations. But your Big Energy is your constant. It is the quiet confidence that comes from within, the deep knowing that you are enough. So the next time fear, doubt, or impostor syndrome creeps in, ask yourself:

- What is this feeling trying to teach me?
- How can I respond with courage and curiosity, rather than resistance?
- How can I reconnect with my Big Energy in this moment?

Remember: it is not about being fearless. It is about moving forward even when fear is present, trusting that your Big Energy will guide you every step of the way. Because when you lead from this place, you are unstoppable.

The Guides on Birth and Death

'The perfect kind of human does not exist.
Each one has its own flaws, and this is what
makes them perfect. For it is these flaws
that gives them a journey to embark on,
collecting the various aspects of themselves
back to wholeness.

When you were born, your journey
already lay ahead of you to trace these
steps of spiritual evolution, back to your
true aspects. So, you see, the human journey
in itself is a rebirth.

Although it is quite easy to see it as a journey
to which you are born, grow, and die, this is
not actually the case. The process of death is
the birthing into your next form; to what you
really are.

Life is continually rebirthing itself, of which you are part of the process. In and out, round and round, like the seed that grows into a plant, that in turn grows seeds, which grow to die, from which it's seeds grow to be plants yet again.

Each an aspect of each other in different incarnations.

On this journey of continuous incarnations, we drop and collect facets of ourselves, but the end result of death is almost the same emergence into one's true state - the soul aspect, before we then reincarnate to human form to start the journey all over again.

You may wonder why this is a continuous loop. Does it ever stop?

Yes, it does, as there are many diverse levels of existence, distinct levels of consciousness. Angels, ascended masters, spirit guides, humans, and animals are all different states that are incarnated.

As you grow, so do you progress into these forms. And it is rare to regress, unless the soul chooses this course itself. It is more common for a soul to repeat the human journey over and over again, until he

or she completes its dharma (the soul's ultimate purpose or path of evolution, its sacred duty in this lifetime, unique to each being).
Then staying home in its true spiritual form, guiding others on the human journeys. To reach this level, you need to have evolved spiritually into the states required.

However, for some, they get lost on the human journey as they lose sight of the real image and true meaning of life, and so they repeat the human journey over and over again.'

The Guides - Speaking Your Truth Without Fear

'What are you afraid to say?

Your words are an expression of your dynamic, energetic vibrations, when spoken from the depth, of which you truly are, your soul.

The chords of every vibration come together to make what you refer to as the physical.

When you go beyond the senses of sight
to see with your inner compass, your words
become the visible parts of that ultra sensory
world into which you have tapped.

Speak your words from the depth of
your being, and feel its vibration.

Feel it within your cells, as it repurposes,
repositions, and revives your very being.

Your words are the chords that link your internal
world to the physical; so use them with purpose,
intention, and power. This is our message for
you today for we see you are stuck in words, in
expression. Get unstuck.'

Going Forward - Food for thoughts
How Dharma/ Your Purpose
Ties into Your Big Energy

Many people struggle to step into their Big Energy
because they are unknowingly fighting against their
dharma. It is often said that we are most afraid of our
own power, and our dharma is a super power! Instead
of aligning with our soul's highest path, we often get
caught up in external expectations, fear, or distractions

that pull us away from our true purpose.

When you are disconnected from your dharma, you may feel:

- Drained or unfulfilled, even if you are 'successful.'
- As if you're spinning your wheels, working hard but not making real progress.
- Lost or stuck in repeating cycles, facing the same struggles over and over again.
- Uncertain about your next steps, questioning your decisions or doubting yourself.

But when you align with your dharma, your Big Energy naturally expands because you are operating from a place of deep truth. Life feels more synchronised, opportunities flow more effortlessly, and even challenges become stepping stones rather than roadblocks.

Your Dharma and Big Energy Are Already Within You

Dharma is not something you need to find, it is already within you, waiting to be remembered. Your Big Energy is your natural, limitless force, but it is most powerful when you are in harmony with your purpose.

The question to ask yourself is:

'Am I fighting against my dharma or flowing with it?'

Because Big Energy is not just about manifesting more, it's about manifesting what is truly meant for you.

We will dive more into purpose in Chapter 9.

CHAPTER 7
Harnessing Energies & Elements

One of the most powerful ways to step fully into your Big Energy Pants is by learning to harness the energies and elements that surround us and exist within us. These creative forces are not separate from who we are; they are woven into the fabric of our being. Our ability to manifest, to create, and to live with purpose lies in recognising and working with these energies consciously.

At the heart of this creative process are the masculine and feminine energies. These are not tied to gender, they are universal forces that exist within everyone, regardless of being male or female. They also flow through everything in the universe. Together, they are the ultimate power source beneath our ability to turn vision into reality. These two energies complement each other, forming the foundation of creation itself. The interplay between them is what makes manifestation not just possible, but effortless when balanced.

The masculine and feminine energies are the essential components of creativity, each playing a distinct yet harmonious role in the process. **Feminine**

Energy is the energy of healing, intuition, and nurturing. It represents receptivity, the ability to lean back, and the art of *being*. It holds space for vision, creation, and sustenance. Feminine energy is not to be forced or tamed; its power lies in allowing it to flow naturally. **Masculine Energy** is the energy of action, structure, and movement. It represents *doing*, bringing ideas and visions into tangible form. The masculine energy is driven, determined, and focused.

Together, these energies create life. The feminine holds the vision, the intuition, and the space for creation to arise, while the masculine brings movement, structure, and action to manifest that vision into reality.

Balancing these energies is where the magic lies. Too much of one without the other leads to imbalance. When the **masculine dominates**, we find ourselves in overdrive; constantly *doing* without rest or reflection. This can lead to exhaustion, overwhelm, and even burnout.

When the **feminine is neglected**, there is no space to heal, replenish, or align with our intuition. Creativity becomes forced, and our efforts feel disconnected from our purpose. Equally, if the feminine energy becomes overly dominant, leaning too far into stillness and reflection without action, the result can be stagnation or a lack of progress.

Both energies are necessary, but they must work in harmony. The feminine energy nurtures, sustains, and aligns, while the masculine energy drives, builds, and delivers. Without the feminine ability to heal and sustain, the masculine drive becomes overpowering and unsustainable.

When you learn to balance and consciously use these energies, you tap into an incredible power tool for manifesting with ease. This is not about forcing one energy to dominate over the other. Instead, it is about allowing them to dance together, each playing its unique role in the creative process.

The masculine requires patience and understanding. It is a force of determination and action, but it must work in tandem with the feminine to avoid becoming destructive or overwhelming. Similarly, the feminine must be allowed to lean back and simply *be* without fear of being overrun.

The key to harnessing these energies is awareness. Ask yourself:

Am I leaning too heavily into doing, without allowing myself to rest and recharge? Am I holding back in reflection and waiting, without taking the inspired action needed to move forward?

As you explore these energies, you will begin to notice how they show up in your personal and professional life. You will recognise when you are leaning too far into the masculine: overworking, overcontrolling, or pushing too hard. You will also see when you are staying too long in the feminine, waiting for things to align without taking the necessary steps to bring them to life.

Through this balance, you will find the key to creating with flow and ease. You will learn to work smarter, not harder, and to align your efforts with the natural rhythms of your being and the universe itself.

Harnessing the energies and elements is not just about manifesting what you want, it is about living in harmony with yourself, aligning with your purpose, and stepping fully into your Big Energy.

The Guides on the Rise and Fall of the Masculine and Feminine

'You have an influenced script in what you have been told.

When the world/your planet was created, it was with both sides of the feminine and masculine. It was created on the assumption of creating balance.

You cannot have balance without two equal aspects. Although it seems like as time has progressed, one aspect gained more power, the masculine.

And this has influenced how society
has grown, underpinned by ego and greed.

Which are both masculine energies.

The more this side of energy gained power,
the more it influenced the script.

We have watched from afar the speed
of such imbalance.

But just like everything else, everything
needs to give back to the opposite side
when one side is too heavy.

The feminine is needed to heal any
damage that may have occurred
during these centuries of the masculine
claiming power.

And to do that she must also
rise to claim power.

But not in the way of the masculine.

She is more tenacious in her approach.

Humans are not necessarily these energies, but more a part of it, so they play their part in this balance.

One can easily move between both of these energies, and balance is also important to maintain in oneself and not lose oneself to either of the energies.

On the physicality, every woman is to be protected and cherished by the man, and, in the same vein, there are some women that are never to be hurt by the man. These are the women here to do God's work.

For if a man is lucky enough to walk the journey with her, he should make it his purpose to create space for her to do God's work. 'Honour her as a woman.'

And if he is unlucky to lose her in ungodly ways, he shall forever walk his path like a lost soul, for he can never find the gift he once had in awakening his own soul.'

The Guides on the Energies and the Elements

'The elements from which you are made
are the same that surround you, which
means you are everything and everything
is you. Nothing is separate.

You can transform this element and so can it you.

In the beginning were only the elements,
with the power of the opposites of forces,
what you call the masculine and feminine,
came transmission of the soul into the human
embodiment. Thus allowing the soul to feel
physically what the elements here on Earth feel....

...to the soul, nothing is perceived as
good or bad. Just a journey of experiences.
It is the physical human experiences that
have labelled it so in line with the ego aspect
of the human form.

So now there is you as the soul, limitless in
potential, because it is the energy of God.'

The Guides on Soul Conversations

'There is another type of language we
have that many are not aware of. A web
of energy transmissions that is of feelings,
states, and mirroring.

This language also includes what we are
reflecting on the outside of us; what we call reality.
It is an engagement between the self and the
universal energy and it is constantly in motion.

If you could see it with the naked eye, it would
be like a wave of translucent light colours,
moving like that of the **Aurora.**

Many people are very surface, for they see
only the reflection of what they are putting out
into their physical reality and therefore have
forgotten how to read the real language.

This language is universal across souls, and
what people sometimes term as feelings. It is
the language each of our souls is still using to
commune with each other without the physical
aspect being aware.

To commune, they do this on an energetic
plane, where neither time nor object exist.
Where only truth, light and love is all.

On this plane anything is possible, and
when in your human experience and you
are able to tap into this aspect of communication,
you go to the roots of anything to align it back;
every time you emerge, your physical state is
like a newborn.'

The Guides on Creative Energy

'The ultimate creative feminine energy
is Mother Earth herself. You can see feminine
features within her. The roundness of her
shape, the waves of her ocean, the cycles of
the seasons, her creativity, and different
moods, never constant, always moving,
forming, taking shapes.

This is the feminine energy that is the creative
life force that births everything and it is the
beholder of all you see. As an aspect of this
energy, every embodiment of the feminine

energy e.g. the woman or man in touch with this aspect of themselves, holds the responsibility in continuing to co-create life. Therefore, a woman who shies away from her feminine essence restricts herself from her purpose and her connection to Mother Earth herself.

On the other hand, venturing on a journey to deepen your connection to this energy, you lay open a catalyst of powerful abilities that currently lie dormant within you.

There are many ways to evoke within you this potent creative life force energy that is the feminine; you only have to look at Mother Earth and all her representations to integrate into the various aspects of her.'

✳

Chapter Exercises
A Creative Life Force Integration Practice
From today, start to observe the several ways you feel that Mother Earth shows up for you. Try to incorporate symbols, the elements, the feelings, and the characteristics and put together your own magical chest of collections: be it physical, written, or mental images for each aspect.

Know what it means for you and how it represents the feminine aspect of the energy we speak about, then slowly start to practise using each and every one in your day-to-day reality.

For example, we know water is a powerful element of Mother Earth. Water holds memories, changes shape, flows, cleanses, and has power. In fact, it is a major component of your own physical composition. Knowing this, can you work more with this element?

It is common for humans to stop seeing things for what they really are. Most people know they need water to survive and take this into their bodies very unconsciously, as only a means to live.

Could you today change your approach and become more conscious, knowing every time you take in you this powerful element, you connect even further to an aspect so powerful, and in so doing you have within you her abilities as well?

When you drink consciously, feel into the healing and cleansing properties, and become one with it.

You can also pre-charge your water with your intentions and desires, because this element holds energy.

*

Connecting with the Elements (Nature) using the Energy of Love and Compassion for Higher Knowledge

If you ever get the chance in nature, find a quiet space, and evoke this energy in you by connecting with your heart. Go into a state of compassion and love, where the ego does not come into play. In this state, approach a tree of your liking, ask it for permission to enter its store of knowledge and wait for a response.

If you feel it open up to your approach, you can either face it with your hands round it, like a hug or sit quietly on its roots, with your back rested upon its trunk. In this position, let go of all and go into a meditative state where you surrender and trust that you are held and protected.

Evoke more of these feelings of compassion and love in you, and in this connection, you are now established with this divine being, for that is what trees are.

Now, listen with the heart; you would be amazed at what is downloaded to you in this process.

After you finish your communion with this being, thank it with sincerity for the gifts and bring yourself back fully into your body making sure you take your time to fill all aspects of your physical body and then feel yourself grounded by Mother Earth.

Not only are you now with wisdom, but you will also feel renewed with new energy, purpose and power.

*

Prayer & Affirmation: Using the Elements to Clear Emotional Blocks

Here is a simple prayer that has worked for me and my clients:

'I call upon the elements to break down all blockages, all stuck energy to clear any negative entities, energy and thoughts as I open the flow of abundance in wealth, health, alignment, ease, flow, beauty and pure consciousness in all I do, all that I am, and all that surrounds me.'

*

PART THREE

CREATE IT:

Consciously Create
the Life You Desire

CHAPTER 8

Manifesting What You Desire

In this chapter we dive into how to align with our true desires and manifest them into reality through spiritual principles and the law of attraction, as the Guides say...

'Anything is possible, but only if you
believe it is. The way of creativity is only but this.
Your ability to create anything in your life lies
in the level of trust you have in yourself and
who you truly are.

When you start to realise that everything you
perceive around you is only a thought form,
then you will realise that what makes everything
feel so solid are the beliefs you hold around the
vision of all that you perceive.

Nothing is as solid as you see it.

Although the more you identify with the
human aspect of your current experience, the
more physical and permanent they will seem.

And this is because this is the purpose of the human journey: to experience the physical reality of life.

However, your ability to make anything possible in your life comes from your spiritual state; for here you are able to see the smoke and mirrors, and use your natural ability to mould whatever you desire.'

I love this download.

A reminder that whatever you put energy into, will start to grow and manifest in your life. So, it can be said that your life is a manifestation of where you have been investing your energy and that everything you see up to this point in your reality is a sum of where you have been investing or directing your energy.

Many people are unaware of this and are subconsciously creating a life they do not want.

They focus so much on what they do not want in an attempt to avoid it, and, instead, they keep manifesting it.

This is why the concept of clarity - knowing what you want and how to focus on it - is so important.

A wonderful way to do this, is to make an effort to figure out your purpose in life (your dharma like we previously navigated), as this becomes a catalyst of giving us direction towards a more fulfilling state of being, like a map or compass.

When you know what you want, things will start to happen, and in the majority of the cases you never even know the 'how' it will come to be.

Have you noticed how sometimes things may feel so 'this way' and the next day, things can totally change to the opposite? For instance, once, I was speaking to a friend of a friend who was telling me about a time in her life when they were desperate to move house, they had mould in the house, the space was in a bad state, she had no job and she could not find anything within her and her boyfriend's budget.

One day she got so fed up, she could take it no more; she just knew they had to move. That night she went online (to the same site she has searched everyday) only to find a perfect place within their budget, and within that same period an offer of a job.

I agree with the school of thought that alternate realities exist; one which is happening simultaneously and one which we can jump between different realities of ourselves. We do it repeatedly, and I believe the thing that powers us to jump reality is the force of the energy behind it.

We go through a painful or sublime situation that creates the energetic power needed to ultimately break through one energetic vibration (reality) to the other. Whether you are willing to take that energy to push forward or sink deeper into a rut is another story. It is also possible to jump realities in a more conscious way.

One which we power ourselves using the various tools available to us to light us up from within.

One where we are using a higher vibration rather than those caused by 'situations' which generate a low vibration energy. This is where I think, spirituality, meditation, dance, music, sensual energy etc. comes into play. These tools activate our senses so much that we are left with our 'real essence' through polarisation. This is essentially what we use to move through alternate realities; especially when it happens with a bang towards our heart's desires. Regardless, it is important to remember that when we jump realities, we are jumping to a place of intention (conscious or unconscious ones). What are your intentions? Think of the times when you have found things have dramatically changed in a certain situation; it is usually because you have become so transfixed on your intention for a change.

A game changer for me was the realisation that everything we need and everything we create is within us. Not just knowing the theory but really coming to understand this concept.

The knowing that we create our own realities and that we as human beings are an exact replication of the universe is powerful. Everything exists within us and our outer world is really only a reflection of our inner world.

Yet, we have been conditioned to see our creation process, and the manifesting of it, as something that is external from us. When we seek to create financial security for ourselves and our families, we see that as a process which can only be achieved by getting out there and chasing the thing we feel will give it to us.

When we feel lonely and desire love in our lives, we chase after a partner or sexual gratification because we feel this is where our fulfilment comes from. I talk about our search for love as a means of finding ourselves in chapter ten.

When our health falls short of what it should be, in most cases we go for treatment after treatment, looking for that fix. The list goes on…

When we come to realise that we as 'beings' are indeed a sample of the universe in all its form, we come to realise that we create and are transforming just exactly as things are creating within the cosmic realm, if on a minute scale.

Our ability to dig deep and go within to first work on our inner world, is the game changer in leading a life of flow and magic. I always say: 'abundance is a state of mind.' This is why the concept of mantra and affirmation works. However, many use these tools without actually knowing why and how they work. They need to understand that these are tools which help shape the configuration of our inner world.

Each mantra and affirmation carries its own energetic frequency, which helps re-structure our own internal configuration, which in turn creates the outer realities we desire, by helping us align with the right frequency.

They say everything is energy, right? So, if we think about everything around us in that form, it is much easier to align yourself to that which we seek. Love is energy and universal frequency. To have more love in your life, you first need to accept and realise you are love. How can you then go chasing that which you already are? When we accept we are love, and use this as the foundation for everything we do, we attract love to us. Like attracts like.

This same principle applies to everything. Let us take abundance as an example. Many people want more money, they want more opportunities, they want to create security etc.

The first step towards all these things we seek is to realise that abundance is a state of mind, and therefore a state of being. This again is an 'inside job.' The process of having an abundant mindset comes with the ability to trust that you are always going to be taken care of and to learn to surrender. When we learn these two things, we learn how to go with courage (rather than fear) and learn to take steps inspired by our intuition. We create with ease because we know we can, and go after what is truly, divinely, ours.

The process of creating or manifesting may not always look like we thought it would. But this is what I talk about by learning to trust and surrender. So, for example, the way you thought that the money you needed to buy that house would come to you, turns out differently from the way it happens.

You thought, and had it all planned, that you were going to get a job that pays £xxx and then you will get a mortgage in xxx months. But looking back at how you bought that house, looks nothing like how you had envisaged it, but you still got your heart's desires.

It could be that all of a sudden a family member left you some money or in the end you were able to even access a loan (which you never thought of), or perhaps even an opportunity arose for you to take up a friend's house (perfect to your needs), whilst he or she travelled around the world.

This is why, when creating your realities, you need to be open to the manner in which your dreams come to reality. By not being too fixed on the 'how' puts us in the mindset of being open to the unusual ways it could come to be. In everything we do, we should be intention-driven and be more flexible in the how.

I once had a client who came into my world in a very, shall we say, desperate time. She was about to be homeless with a child, had no money, and also desired a car to be able to achieve her motherly duties. When we spoke about her situation – logically - it felt like it was an impossible position. And yet within a week, her reality transformed. She got not just a home, and the car, but also launched her coaching business.

You are love, you are light, you are an expansive being. You are a creative and spiritual being, and your manifesting abilities are beyond what your physical eyes can see.

Whilst such things as vision boards and goal setting may help you direct focus towards an intention, it is important at times to also open up to the possibility that these are limiting you.

This is why it is important to use detachment. Come from a place where you are open to divine possibility as you walk this path towards your desires. This way you open to bigger possibilities than you can ever imagine. Doing this takes courage and surrender in moments of chaos or challenges, as you are driven to bigger things.

Prayer:
A Prayer and Affirmation in Times of Worry:

'Today I put my trust in God.

The realisation that I have been in a more troublesome situation and survived, reminds me that I am always looked after. I am always supported.

And so, I choose to not panic nor worry about what may come to be or not to be, while I ease through this current shift.

I trust that all will be well.

*I trust that my angels are always supporting me,
and I trust I am exactly where I need to be.*

*While I trust and surrender, I settle within
myself and drop the need for struggle and the
cycle of hardship.*

*I drop the energy of lack, for now I know that I
am always provided for and that everything is
within my reality.*

*I choose flow, I choose ease, I choose abundance,
I choose wealth, I choose love, I choose expansion,
I choose beauty, and I choose alignment and pure
consciousness*

*(you can replace a vibrational word
with one that feels more aligned to you).*

I am safe.

And so, it is.'

This type of prayer and affirmation works when they are
spoken from the heart with all humbleness; for in the
heart, the ego has no place.

Speak from your heart and ask with your heart. This is the path to what you want.

When you go through your heart you go directly to the core of all energetic resonance.

The heart has the power to activate not just yourself but everything around it. Its vibration is that of the vibration of creation itself. In fact, it is of the same thing.

So when you choose the path of the heart, you are at the core of it all, and have and know how to activate what you want, for this is your creative work.

A person with a blocked heart resists receiving from the universe, for they cannot vibrate at its resonance. The heart is what links you to it all. However, a person with an awakened heart is open and connected, and this person is powerful.

As I take time to write now, I speak from and through the heart, which also means I speak to your heart. This essentially has the power to activate your own heart. So, you see, the power of your heart centre lies not just in receiving from source but in activating everything: your relationship, creativity, abundance, and healing.

Your heart is the key to the answer you seek.

Spend every day nurturing and acknowledging your heart centre, and in this way you will become attuned to it. You will become a more activated being who is powerful and manifested of all things that are in alignment to the real aspect of you: light and love.

*

Exercise to Open the Heart to Receiving

Take a moment to connect with your heart as you read this. Place both hands on your heart centre or right hand on the chest (heart centre), left hand on the lower part of your abdomen.

Close your eyes and take three deep breaths in and out. Connect with your heart and in your mind's eye, imagine a circle of white light vibrating outwards from your heart centre.

Keep breathing deeply into your heart centre and repeat this mantra:

'I am open to receiving.'

Repeat the mantra over and over as you stay in your heart centre.

This simple practice is both a healing (unblocking your heart) and an activation. If you feel any discomfort, fear or panic (which can sometimes happen), ground yourself by feeling your feet rooted to the ground, and continue with the mantra.

How to Make Anything Possible

Anything is possible if only you believe it is. If you do, you are able to direct energy towards what you want through FOCUS. This is what materialises your desires into reality.

In my work with women, one of the biggest issues usually centres around finding the focus to do what is required to achieve their dreams.

There are many ways different people go about doing this. Making big yearly goals is one of the most popular ones, and also the main reason for the downfall of their desires.

Finding the focus to do anything is an energy like anything else.

Over the years, the way I make goals for the years to come has changed. I have not been one to make specific goals anyway, as I always found it did not align with how I operate. So, I would rather use a 'feeling' and get clear on the different ways that feeling could be evoked.

I found that we can limit ourselves when our 'goals' are so defined to a tee, because in this way, we are working along the lines of our limited ego. Because we cannot conceive how much bigger a potential and magical way things can come to be, we restrict ourselves to what we view as possible.

I remember a time in the beginning of my manifestation mastery journey, when I calculated that in order to feel what I wanted to feel for that year, I needed a quarter of a million pounds; to be specific it was £240,000. I then made the intention in the months of December to bring in £240,000 for the following year. In January of the following year I received £245,000 in two different blocks.

Except, I received it in a unique way and a different purpose from what I had in mind. The money came for a property investment opportunity I had called in.

You see, the universe does not care what your specific goals are, or how your intentions come to be, she rather listens to the vibration you emit, in other words she matches your feelings.

And she is so much more powerful than what your mind can ever conceive.

Which means your potential is so much bigger than what your logical mind feels you can create or achieve as set in your 'goals.'

So how about we keep ourselves focused and expansive by making a commitment to how we want to feel, be supported, and show up?

How about we dare to have a bigger context for our lives, and give a bit of space for the universe to do her magic? And if you are worried time is passing you by to do all these, here is what the guides say in our dialogues.

I worried I was not going fast enough, that I lost momentum with part of my spiritual purpose. And I was told this by my guides...

'There is nothing to rush for when you rush
you work to your own timeline.

We do not work to this time.

It is the human perception that makes time
what it is, so when you worry if you are going
fast enough, this is a false perception.

We move by the puzzle, the putting together
of each piece.

This, you could say, is our time.

And the energy is what dictates the movement, i.e.
when something will fit or when it is in holding.

We move more only by the movement of the
puzzle fitting together.

You can then say intention is our only purpose,
and by which we measure movement.

The coming together of pieces coming to whole.

This is the same for who you are, and your time in
your human experiences is a journey of bringing
the pieces together to come back to whole.

Your journey is a puzzle.

So, worry not about time, for that is a false illusion created as part of the ego's will for control.

Focus more on the pieces of yourself that you are here to collect and bring together, for the whole universe is a combination of this work.'

CHAPTER 9

The Journey to Finding Your Purpose

Poem - Who am I? What is My Purpose?

I woke up one morning during my most challenging time of my life and was filled with these words, which is befitting to start this chapter:

'Who have I become, where I am going?

I contemplate life's purpose, its mysteries, its challenges.

I feel… cry, laugh aloud.

I stare at the stars, moon, and salute the sunrise.

I touch leaves, feel the wind on my face, chase thunder, walk barefoot.

I dance naked, laugh at my challenges, take the mickey out of my anger.

*I go for days without food or the spoken words, I
dive and hide away in my deepest shadows.*

I follow my heartbeat, listening to its whispers.

Who am I? What is my purpose?

*I am wild, untamed, spirit, infinite, power,
energy, divine being, God's presence*

Manifesting my heart desires.'

One of the most frequent questions I get asked is: 'How do I find my purpose?'

The search for purpose, I was once told by a very wise and spiritual man I met in Portugal, is like going down the rabbit hole. Sometimes you think you have found something, and sometimes it leaves you feeling empty, making space for you to fill yourself with what you are truly meant for.

I believe the journey to finding and stepping into your true purpose is not a logical one, and therefore not something that anyone can prescribe with a step-by-step, one size fits all guide. However, what I will do is to tell you my story, of how I eventually stepped into *my* purpose, doing this energy work where my true gift lives.

The journey of finding one's purpose, I believe, is constantly unravelling, and mine has always been interlinked with the call to visit a particular place. In each of these places, it always felt I unlocked another layer to my knowledge, gifts, insight, and the essential deeper clarification of what my purpose is.

One of my first deep calls was to Bali (and yes, like every other 'Live, Laugh, Love' kind of girl, you are sniggering!). Well… perhaps!

One day, I spontaneously packed a backpack and headed to Bali. By spontaneous, I mean I went for lunch one day in London Victoria and felt called to walk into a travel agent. I came out with a flight to Bali. I had never visited before and did not know what to expect. I booked only my first night's accommodation and trusted that I would be divinely guided. It turned out to be one of those experiences I will probably be telling my children, their children (and you) until everyone is tired of hearing it.

Bali, March 2017

I can best illustrate my experience in Bali by a piece I wrote for The Huffington Post titled 'Why Bali is Not a Good Idea', written from the perspective of the ego. It was rejected and never published, which was disappointing, although I did get an intuitive nudge that I needed sovereign power over this for my own purpose, so I guess that is what they meant, using it here in my own book. Here goes - rough and raw as I journal it out then…

∽∾

'Dear Bali,

You are a bad idea. People, please do not go there.

I went to Bali for time out… you know, to clear my head and figure out what I really wanted to do with my life when I grow up.

Now I just do not want to do anything, and then I want to do everything. You really got me all confused.

You know, some of my friends back in England were not ready to come to you because we have this thing called 'beach bod ready'. But me, no… I did not listen.

I came with all my curves. Did you care? No! Your men did not give a damn. They were too busy asking me where I am from, how I spell my name, calling me beautiful or Nelson Mandela (like I knew him personally) and in Gili Islands, they ALWAYS sang 'Waka Waka' to me (a quote from a song).

And your women, they were too busy trying to sell me an exquisite sarong or trying to make me relax and feel beautiful with their amazing massage and spas. I mean, who needs all that in this busy world of trying to see everything you have to offer. I have travelled too far.

You were really a bad idea, Bali.

Now, do not even get me started on your food. I have eaten so much of it, I am just grateful for your sun; for at least in my head, I am sweating some of that weight-gain off. Perhaps I should have waited to come to you with a 'beach ready bod'.

I love travel. I travel to seek spirituality and soul expansion; with you my thirst for travel has heightened. Who is going to fund that? You? Bali?

But seriously everything here feels so spiritual, the people, the food, the art... so much so that everything feels sacred like you should only capture it with your heart....

Now this is really affecting my ego. I love photography. How do I show my people just how good a picture I can capture of you, if I am limited to just a few, and savour the best in my heart?

Talking about heart – I am not sure how you do it, but I keep having these experiences of heart expansion. There was the time I cried in one of your water temples and the time you insisted I meet everything in my life (love, business, relationships) from a soul level, like I do with my spirituality. It takes humility, vulnerability and following my emotions... that is scary, I say.

I am reminded about my judgemental character, when I express my views about certain things which illustrate the easiness of the Balinese, as they easily laugh it off. You are spiritual, yet 'everything goes' with your children.

I once read that vibrators are not allowed in Indonesia (do not ask me how I know that... ahem!), but you have the penis on display everywhere you look. Okay I get it, perhaps it's to do with Shiva... but still!

I know now, you are not for me, Bali.

It has been amazing for both my masters though... as it has been a heart and soul activation, as both seem to be expanding in happiness in your presence.

Thanks a lot Bali, I am bruised, shattered, and diminished. But I understand.

In fact, this lady I met on my last day in Ubud, phrased it perfectly, "Bali is not the place to go with a plan, it's the place to just turn up and see what opens up." That can be pretty hard for someone like me.

Sincerely,

The ego.'

∽∞∾

I tell you what opened up for me in Bali; I came back home a different person. The transformative experience in Bali, was where delivering the practice of womb work started stirring deep within me.

I returned to the UK and closed the video company that I had just started before heading to Bali - soon after this awakening. It was difficult for me to tell my then new business partner who had invested time and money in our new venture that I could not go ahead any longer with what we had planned. I did not know yet again how I would survive financially or even what I needed to do to move forward. However, I knew I had to step into the courage of following my intuition at that point. For the very first time in my life, I had to bet on myself and my own spiritual gifts.

The initial awakening to step into my spiritual work in Bali led me to the mystical world of 'shamanic-led' energy work, even though at first I feared even the word itself!

I had dived into delivering womb-healing work to women who experienced profound transformation and then came the calling to deepen my ability, supplemented by becoming a breath coach, guiding women through an emotional detox, with just the power of the breath.

Although I must admit, I did not fully step into my purpose and calling until Portugal, a year after Bali.

Portugal - June 2018

For years I had been drawn to go to Portugal. I knew for some reason this was going to be a spiritual trip. It was just a gut feeling. But I had not been given any clues as to when to go or even what to do there.

The first urge I had to go to Portugal was when I went through my bad breakup from the father of my child in 2014.

After the breakup, for some reason I made the decision to move from England to Portugal. I did not know why Portugal, especially as I had never been there before. But I remember being moved in such a way that I started to look at places to rent.

I had no money back then, nor a job, so not even sure how I thought I was going to make that possible. I remember finding a place and almost renting it. I then spoke to my mother about this, who convinced me that this was not the right move.

I let this sit with me for a couple of years, but the urge never went away.

Fast forward to 2018, I got an email inviting me to help with the organising of an ecstatic dance event in Portugal, but for some reason, I never quite made it. It was later that year that I finally made it to Portugal.

That year was a year of profound transformation.

Before making my trip to Portugal, everything around me started to fall apart. It was a challenging time in my life. Everything felt blocked. Money stopped coming in no matter what I did. I could not get clients, nor could I get a contract. I got myself into a position where my accounts returns to Companies House were all late. I had three different companies back then, so you can imagine I was getting notifications from HMRC left, right and centre. I had not paid my corporation tax because, you guessed it, I had not budgeted for it or put it aside.

I got into such a state that I was not fixing anything. I was in fight or flight mode. I was scared to even open my mail, so I just let it pile up. I remember thinking that I would need to sell my house to get back into the flow of things to be able to pay off my debts; I had over £30K in debt.

One morning I walked to my ex-partner's house, deeply contemplating how I would release myself from this state. I spoke to him of my intention to sell my place. He thought I should not, and suggested moving into his for a while, rent out my place to help me get back on my feet, and pay him a few hundred pounds less than my mortgage as rent for my son's bedroom when he stays there.

Not thinking clearly, I said yes, desperate to take any offer of help.

I listed my place on Airbnb the same day, went to sleep, woke up and someone had booked my place for three months!

The only thing she needed was to move in the next

day, and so I found myself frantically packing all our clothes, shoes, and anything else I could take in black bin bags to my ex-partner's; my ex-house.

The whole thing felt like it happened so fast, that it felt surreal. I remember standing in his hallway, surrounded by all the black bin bags, thinking what have I done? How did this happen? How am I back here? At this point I went into a deep surrendering automation mode.

I knew deep within me that I was going through a spiritual awakening, and in this I went into humility, deep prayers, and communion with God in the days that followed.

I asked 'What is my lesson here? Why am I back here?' for I knew this place very well.

And I was told I was here to do the work of forgiving my ex-partner; that I was brought back to be put in an environment to 'do the work.' 'To do the work' is to love, to open my heart and to learn to receive; and so my work started. As I was there, I leaned in.

I allowed him to take care of me in the little ways he knew how, when he offered anything small like a meal. I said thank you, smiled and stayed in my body.

I expressed my truth when I needed to, and felt myself get more grounded with every single day.

By the second or third week, as I was still navigating the heaviness of it, I decided to retreat and go stay at one of my family friend's places with my son for the weekend. They had children the same age as my son, and it always felt like going back home whenever I was there.

There was always African music, they always had tasty food, and it was always good to be there. However, on this visit, things took a turn for the worse, as with everything else that was happening around me at that time. They had a party going. They had friends over and music was playing, and people were drinking. I am not much of a drinker so, after one or two drinks, I really feel the alcohol.

I decided to retreat early, and I went to sleep in the living room. After having a bit to drink at one point, my friend's husband came in and sexually assaulted me. Shocked and confused I stayed up all night, waiting for daybreak to come so that I could leave the house with my son. When daybreak came, the husband was already up playing music in the kitchen singing along and happy as Larry. My stomach was in my throat, and I felt disgustingly sick as I got my son ready to leave.

Of course, he did not know why, all of a sudden, we had to leave a day earlier, nor did my friend (his wife), so I had my son crying saying: 'Why do we have to leave?' And my friend saying, 'I thought you were here for the weekend.'

Returning to my ex-partner, I could not tell him about what had happened as I felt guilty and ashamed of the incident. I could not tell anyone for days, so I went into deep prayers asking yet again, 'What is my lesson in all this?'

All the while, as I contemplated what to do, I was getting texts from my friend's husband begging me not to tell his wife, telling me that if I did, I will be breaking the family up. I felt stuck between wanting to do the right thing and thinking about their children. It weighed heavily on me, not just the decision, but the shame of it all. I felt dirty, I felt that perhaps maybe I lead him on, perhaps it was my fault. And with all this confusion I went deeper and deeper into prayers. I could not talk to anybody.

I communed deeply with nature and dug deep into my shamanic training/work learning tools and practices like soul integration, energy healing, ancestral healing, energy alchemy.

I spent many days in the public park, Clissold Park, North London. It became my sanctuary. I hugged trees, did my Hatha yoga every morning and meditated in this park. It heightened my deepness and spirituality.

I felt myself transforming into a woman I felt I knew a long time ago, and throughout this period I felt a strong connection to my grandmother and my great grandmother, and perhaps the mothers before them.

Unexpectedly one day in the mist of prayers communing with nature, like I normally do, I had this realisation I am meant to speak out not just for me, but for all the women who were never able to speak out. I was meant to voice my voice, and this was part of my healing. With this realisation I contacted my friend and told her what had happened and what her husband had done to me. She was not surprised, I do not think (in fact, if I were to be honest with my feelings, I would say she knew all along), but she did speak to her husband, of what, I will never know.

He tried to contact me, telling me how I am breaking up his family. I blocked him, told him never to contact me again, even though he still tried on different platforms, and I blocked him on every conceivable way he could contact me.

After this, I felt a strange sense of a new level of power within me. I felt a new purpose like something had cleared, and in its place a new purpose had been instilled within me.

Then one day, I woke up and had this clear call to go to Portugal.

I did not have money, but I knew I had to go. And as these things happened, everything fell into place for me to go.

I remember sitting at the desk in front of my laptop in my son's room that I was renting from his father, searching through Airbnb website, trying to find a place. Everywhere was expensive and there was nothing I could afford. I searched for days and could not find anything.

One night I sat yet again in front of the computer, but this time I decided to truly connect and asked for the things that I wanted on this trip. I closed my eyes and revisited my desires. I wanted a place that I could afford, a place that I could rest my head and sleep deeply, a place to rest, a place that will help me connect deeper into the spiritual journey I was embarking on.

When I opened my eyes and went back into the Airbnb website, the most amazing thing happened! Right on the top of the search page was this place. it was just a simple room in a yoga and meditation centre and with the cheapest rate ever. The funny thing was that I had searched for days, and this had never come up. And now, unexpectedly, something that matched my budget and my desire for a restful place was right in front of me. Many of the reviews mentioned how they had had a perfect sleep because it was so quiet and peaceful. Immediately, I sent a request to the owner asking if I could book the place and I got a response saying yes.

I got on the plane to Portugal a few days later, with no clear idea as to what I was going to be doing there, I just knew I was being called to go.

Portugal had a familiarity to it. I had no map or guide, and yet I knew exactly where I had to go every step. Every day, I was instinctively led to places that felt so familiar that I knew in a past lifetime I had been there before. In all my years, I had never felt something like this.

I felt so connected in a deep way that I cannot even put into words. I expressed this to the landlord of the place that I was renting, and he told me of his similar experiences. It turned out he was a spiritual guru and does past life regression.

We talked about spiritual things, and it also turned out that he knew a lot of dragons. The dragon energy had been the energy I was getting familiar with just before I had left London to come to Portugal. There was so much synchronicity on this trip that it left me in awe at times and other times my heart was so filled with joy. The love, the expansion that yet again I cannot even put into words. In Portugal I saw my past and my future and I knew I had been called there for a reason.

When I returned to London, everything started to fall into place yet again. In magical ways that I do not even understand to this day, I was back into my own house and things started moving yet again. It was almost like the reason I left my home, or the reason I thought I could not afford to be in my own home, and the invisible block never existed.

Things just cleared.

This was one of my most profound life experiences that kickstarted my own way of following and stepping into my soul purpose in this lifetime.

Like I say, finding and following your life's purpose is like a journey of going down the rabbit hole filled with the unknown, and at times wonder, magic, and excitement, if we allow the fear and resistance to drop by surrendering just that little bit more.

Wales - May 2023

By this point, I have come to know when I am being called to do my spiritual work and more attuned to the nature of things. This particular time, I knew it was a calling. It was a call to Wales, so I packed my bag, got into my car, and made the long drive to Wales.

As always with this type of calling, the journey, and the drive to Wales was smooth. I booked accommodation in the small town as indicated by my guides. I did not have a travel book or guidebook, everything was planned intuitively.

On my first day in Wales, I was led to walk to the back of the Airbnb house where I was staying. I was led to a hill that had such a powerful energy surge, that the only way I can describe it is being similar to the energy surge I felt at Stonehenge. I was told (by my guides) this is an activation. I sat on this hill for a long time, meditating. Whilst on the hill, I was told to look into my bag; that there was something in there. When I looked. There was a small crystal, a pink rose crystal that I never knew was there. I was told I would need to do something with this crystal at some point.

The land to which I was led is camouflaged in an unassuming place, and yet a place of pure power for those who are attuned to its frequency; a place where the dragons gathered and flew up in the skies. 'Why am I brought here? What is my work here?' I asked.

'You are brought here as part of your journey. You have already been here before as one of us, and now in human form, so you can be all that you are. You carry both your dragon and human, not that you have not always, but increasingly you are awakening. Your awakening will ascend many, many more."

❦

Wales - Journal Entry: 30/07/23

Today I was led to another spot, randomly behind the hill. I was surprised to find a stone circle; 12 stones in total with another stone inside the circle. I made my way into the circle and sat on it, and immediately I was filled with a rush of memories/ feelings of the persecution of women. Memories flooded through me in an indescribable way.

I was told this was the spot at which I was to leave the crystal which I was given the day before. I was told the previous activation with the energy surge was to activate me to do today's work of cleansing the area.

This was earth renewing the energy of the land. I also found a young man in this same area. It was quiet, just the two of us. I walked over to him as he was fetching water from the river down the hill, to bring up the hill to water the planted trees around the stone circle. He said he was Bulgarian, and that he was volunteering to water the plants. I felt this was weird, surreal, but understandable. Here was I, sent to clear the energy of the land and he was the boy sent to nurture it (whether he knew it or not).

I sat in the circle for a long while before planting the crystal.

I returned to the original hill spot and reported that I have done as asked. I could not resist, cheekily asking about my human desires, my purpose, doing this work that I am here for richly, and wishes for my son, my family. And as I left the hill, I sensed my spiritual guides' sense of humour as they funnily said I may just get my xxxx (a desire I shall not share here) in a very teasing way.

∽

Talking about purpose, once I had this interesting dialogue with my Guides…

'More and more are waking up to the task at hand' they said.

'What is this task at hand?' I asked.

A desire to find their purpose, to follow their destiny, even though they yet not know what it is' they answered.

'The thing is, your destiny is your destiny. It cannot be undone. The fear you feel in your heart of having lost it is only but a fear' they added.

'You may at times lose the connection of the real essences of you, but it is always there.'

'When you awake, we awake. You are also our purpose, for through you, we do our work. We are all one.'

'And so?' I asked

'What is my work right now, for I feel so much energy and a sort of knowing and desire to be doing more?'

'Activation of the sleeping ones is still your work. It happens through the activation of you.

You are the channel. It is your light that
will light up others.

You will be okay, do not fear.

You are always taken care of. We will guide you,
just listen with your heart, for it is the portal.'

So, the answer to the question we started this
chapter on: 'How do I find my purpose?' is –
'Connect with your spiritual gift and bet on
yourself.'

The Guides on Your Gift

'There comes a time when all must connect with
their gift.

You may call it *gift,* but we see it more like your
essence.

You see it is what makes the sum of you. This
essence to which you can think of as energy, that
is your physical attribution. The only thing is that
in your physical reality, most have lost focus; lost
touch with their true essence.

This experience of you here is to use this essence, for each one has a piece to add for the completion.

When one is out of touch with their true essence, a misalignment and dysfunction is experienced in their reality; for they are incomplete in how they are manifesting their state here.

Your role here is to light that which helps those out of touch with their completeness.

This is your essence, but we know you are already in touch with it. We however wish for you to fully step into it."

In Closing this Chapter Here is the Message from my Guides after Wales

"Now is your time. You have started being your purpose, all that you have been through has brought you here.

The path was always to hear. It is an exciting time for you. The vision you have seen in the past is now all coming to be. It is like all that you have asked for is all coming to be,

but it is only a case that all which you thought
you were asking for, was already your purpose.

Everything was preparing you to be able to
hold this purpose so you can carry it now;
it is time to celebrate and expand into it. Into
all that is showing up, say yes with courage,
for it is already laid out for you.'

I hope my journey into my own purpose, activates
something in you - as you make your own journey.

Chapter 10

Living an Authentic Life and Finding Happiness:

Living an authentic life begins with taking ownership of your own happiness. It is easy to fall into the trap of believing that external factors such as your relationships, career, possessions, or achievements will provide the joy and fulfilment we seek. But true happiness is an internal state, independent of these things. It is our responsibility to cultivate the joy and peace that already exist within us, not something to be expected from others or external circumstances.

In the pursuit of happiness, most people dream about finding their soulmates, the love of their life, their twin flames, whatever you choose to call it. We see this as someone out there, something that exists outside of us, and when united with this person, we believe we will finally be genuinely happy and fulfilled.

But what if, in truth, the person we search for is already part of us? We search for love when, in fact, we are love itself. The idea of soulmates is something many of us constantly seek, which, upon reflection, is really a search for ourselves.

We manifest and bring into reality versions of ourselves at various stages of life and our journey, depending on the lessons we need to learn and the aspects of ourselves that are dominant at that stage. To seek a soulmate that truly matches your deepest heart's desires is to learn to become that part of your heart's desires.

I encourage my clients to challenge the narrative they tell themselves. Often, we create stories about our lives that reinforce negativity or hold us back. These stories feel like the truth, but they are really just perspectives we have chosen. By rewriting your story, reframing how you view yourself and your experiences, you have the power to change your outlook and transform your life.

It is also essential to enjoy the journey rather than focusing solely on the destination. We often postpone our happiness, thinking, *'When I achieve this goal, then I'll be happy.'* But true fulfilment comes from appreciating every step along the way. Celebrate your efforts, your growth, and the small wins that happen throughout your journey, not just when you reach the finish line.

Self-care, as you know by now, is another vital aspect of living authentically. Prioritise time for yourself; if you do not value your own wellbeing, no one else will. Make sure you create space in your schedule for activities that nourish you and allow you to reconnect with who you are at your core.

Relationships are also key to an authentic life. Cultivate meaningful connections, beginning with your relationship with yourself. When you value and love yourself, you naturally attract positive, fulfilling relationships. This extends to your connections with loved ones, your family, friends, and even your spiritual relationship. Surround yourself with people who support your growth, and be available to nurture these bonds. Just as nature shows us, there is no fruitfulness without relationships.

And just as you are able to do that - have discernment in who you choose to spend your time with - for some people will diminish your energy rather than nurture it.

Lastly, balance is crucial. A fulfilling life is about harmonising work with play. If you focus solely on work, you may find success, but you will miss out on joy and rest. On the other hand, all play, and no work will leave you unfulfilled in other ways.

Striking a balance allows you to experience life holistically, giving you the space to be both productive and joyful. Living authentically means embracing all parts of yourself, valuing your inner joy, and consciously creating a life that reflects who you truly are.

However, many people are unhappy because they worry too much about what others think of them. In the majority of cases, what you think people believe about you is not even how they actually see you. So, what does it matter?

The most important thing is how you see yourself, for that is indeed true, as it is also how you feel about yourself.

Our focus should always be on what brings us inner peace.

When I ask people what they want, I often hear: "I just want to be happy.' I realise that many have forgotten how to be happy. It is our job to find out what we genuinely want. Without knowing what you want, you cannot achieve it, and nothing great happens until you have clarity on your desires, even when they have not yet materialised.

I once had a session with a client who was contemplating leaving her husband. She told me how he was not making her happy, and how she felt he was not even trying. So I asked her: 'What is it that makes you happy in general?'

She took a moment to consider this question and, in the end, was flabbergasted that she could not pinpoint exactly what made her happy. I then turned to her and said: 'How do you expect your husband to make you happy when you, in fact, have forgotten what makes you happy or even how to be happy?'

Happiness, like authenticity, is not something we find outside of ourselves. It is a journey of uncovering, of letting go of what is not true and stepping into what is. It is about becoming the person who knows their own heart, honours their own needs, and shows up in the world as their fullest, most authentic self.

The path to living an authentic life is not about perfection or having it all figured out, it is about choosing to align with who you truly are, one step at a time. It is a dance between knowing yourself and allowing yourself to grow, between holding onto what matters and letting go of what does not.

So, I ask you now:

What would living authentically look like for you?

What would it feel like to live in alignment with your true self?

Take this moment to reflect, and let it be the start of your journey into a life of joy, fulfilment, and authenticity.

The Guides on The Heart And Happiness

'Happiness is a state achieved through the heart - the entity.

To really commune with God (Love), you have to go through the heart.

It is a channel for communication. When we open the heart, your resonance travels, far and wide.

It is also very protective of itself and can easily stay closed. This is why when people are trying to protect themselves, one of the ways they do this is to shut the heart.

But when the heart is shut, essentially you shut yourself out from the world.

The heart works, just like your third eye is spiritual. They are tapped into the power of intuition and seeing beyond your limited physical senses. This is your portal for seeing spiritually as your soul self. The heart is also the catalyst of powering up the different resonances that take you up a vibration. You can call it 'the machine' to start up the physical human engine that you are. When things are not moving for you in your human experience, start with opening your heart.

The heart and the ego cannot work together. One will need to be quietened because they both have different purposes. Although it is much more common for many to be more driven by the ego than the heart, for the ego promises flashy, bright, and sweet experiences (think instant gratification), while the heart is much more subtle, deeper, and much more lasting in its abilities. So many fall to the ego for aid.'

The Guides on Accepting Yourself

'The way to live one's life is to be true to oneself first. To be true to oneself is to be one with it all. When you step into the willingness to accept all that you are, you give yourself permission to be and become.

Many people, over time, have become diluted in their essence because they do not take the time to look at who they truly are and accept all that they are, right here, right now. In doing so, they carry and perceive only what is projected to them externally and act accordingly.

There is nothing congruent in this way of life, and this is one of the main roots of anxiety and depression: the inability to accept oneself while simultaneously trying to control what is external to you.

Oneness is a word that originates from the same meaning as seeing, acknowledging, and accepting it all, just as it is. It is your role to decide when to choose to accept all that you are. Until that moment, you will walk the path of the unknown and of others, rather than your own.

You could say the route to awakening is
one that leads you to this acceptance of oneness;
of being at peace with it all, just as it is. It is
knowing who you are, what you stand for, and
accepting not only yourself as you are but also
others around you, even when they do not
align with your expectations.

For this acceptance of oneness is the
understanding that everything is exactly as
it should be in this present moment.'

The more I do this work, the more I have come to
understand that authenticity comes from knowing who
you truly are.

This is me: I am She. I am He. It is the realisation that
my guides are all aspects of me. The spirit guides, the
animal spirits, and to God, of whom I am a reflection.

In this way, the knowledge is always here; the
resources are already within me. All it takes is a
reconnection to this aspect of myself and for me to
operate from there. They are not separate. I am that
which I pray to. I am that which I seek for guidance.

I am the wise woman, the divine, the feminine, and
the masculine. Because they are aspects of me and are
within me, I am able to reach inside and tap into these
abundant resources.

When you pray to God or become a channel of God's divinity, you hear the voice within clearly. Many people pray, seeing God as a separate entity, when really, you should look within to hear clearly.

The heart of God is the heart you hold within yourself. You only need to reach inside to hear its voice. If you go seeking God or love outside yourself, you remain lost.

You are that which you seek.

To embody and awaken to who you truly are, it is good practice to start opening the heart. Anything that activates the heart is like an amplifier for God's voice and guidance within you. A blocked heart is a blocked path to God in all its glory.

Chapter Conclusion

In conclusion, what I have realised over the ten-year journey illustrated in this book, is that what gives us peace is inner happiness, that deep knowing that we are following a life of purpose. Anything that contributes towards inner peace is worth doing.

On this journey towards finding my own inner peace, I have come a long way. In January of 2020, just before lockdown, it felt as though everything was bringing me to this point. I mustered up the courage to leave my one bed flat in London and got my son and I a beautiful three bed house right by the water in Hertfordshire. Leaving behind the life I had known for almost all my life, for one I was not sure what awaited us.

Three days before my move day, I got one of the clearest direct downloads I have ever had, from my spirit guides, from whom you have been hearing throughout this book.

It said:

'What an amazing life, Folake.

You are truly on purpose, doing what you went back to do. We feel excited you have finally awakened for we have been waiting for quite a while for your arrival.

There is much to do, and time is of the essence. We have set the path for you and things are in motion. There is not much for you to worry about, for all that is will unfold for you. You can feel it in your heart, just follow its drumming and its lead.

Your path is big, and your purpose is huge. There is no going back. What we need you to do now is to step into the hugeness. All that you currently desire will help you along this path. So, follow those desires, stay grounded and in the moment, and the tribe you are of will show up, for it is your destiny.

> Trust and remember who you are.
>
> We are always with you.'

There are tears as I write this to you in this book, because I know by you reading this - my blessings are your blessings too.

*

Chapter Exercises
Meditation for Being at Peace with it All:

Take a moment today to sit quietly and feel back into your body, your breath, the sensations within you, the position in which you sit, where you sit, the environment you are in, the landscape around you, the people, your current situation and who you are being.

Expand your consciousness into all these areas in this exact same step and just be at peace with it all, without judgement or attachment; knowing it is exactly as it should be.

Stay in this energy of meditation for at least 15 minutes. When you are done, step into a state of gratitude for the seeing, acceptance and blessings of this moment and go about your day in this energy.

This simple practice - if repeated over and over again - brings you back into oneness that is everything. Where everything is only but a reflection of everything else.

When you are aligned with this energy of oneness, it is difficult for anyone to knock you off your pedestal, for you are at peace with it all just as it is, and at one with the universal energy.

*

'This is Me'

Look at yourself in the mirror without judgement, but rather in acceptance of every feature that you are and see. Take time to do this.

Love the human you are given. Be at peace and at one with him/her.

Looking at every feature with love, compassion, and acceptance.

Then when you are ready, say silently in your mind this affirmation:

> *This is me.*
> *I am s/he*
> *I am love*
> *I am all*
> *I am*

*

Closing Chapter

Ella, Sri Lanka
December 2024

So, here is where this book finds me and where we conclude this first part of our journey together. This last closing finds me in the beautiful and lush country of Sri Lanka. Yet another calling to visit a land for my spiritual journey – but this time unlike all the ones I have mentioned in this book. This trip feels like it is to nurture my own soul.

On the trip, there has not been any spiritual instructions to heal any part of the land or to do any specific spiritual work (like in my other travels) – which is all great, because the people here in Sri Lanka feel very much in their happy place – like 'at home' - very symbolic of the state we aspire for - along our journey together.

I feel a sense of surrender to receive as I sit staring at one of the most beautiful, lush, and green mountain landscapes I have ever laid eyes on. Right in front of me are tall trees reaching for the clouds, with views of Adam Peak, Ella Rock and to its side the magnificent view of Ravana Falls (waterfall).

Every morning here, I make sure to rise for sunrise to watch it rise against this beautiful landscape and every day I sit in solitude and in deep gratitude and contentment doing absolutely nothing but just taking the views in.

I am staying at an ancient Buddhist temple that felt like the perfect sanctuary I needed to complete this book (away from the noise of the world). A Bodhi tree sits behind me on the grounds of this monastery, protected and held in reverence and to its side - the temple. I have joined the monks in prayers and meditation and made friends with the little monks in training (age roughly seven to ten years old), who often stand next to me as I type away!

The journey to Sri Lanka has been nothing but effortless, although the first week I fell ill – a much-needed purification of the body I sense. I have travelled my way from Colombo along the coast to Negombo where the Sri Lankans have made me feel at home, travelling through to Unawatuna all the way to Ella (where I write this). Tomorrow, the journey will then take me to Kandy and back to Negombo and then Colombo.

There have been lots of synchronicities, like signs showing me I was on the right track. I have not had to plan much for this trip to Sri Lanka, because I have been intuitively guided along the way – with people and places (just like the Monastery) showing up to give this journey such an enriching experience. I feel at home in my body, grounded, happy, feminine, with a kind of vitality and a sense of power bubbling within me.

The head monk at the monastery gave me a special blessing. In the blessing he wished me luck on my work, the book, acknowledging my 'greatness' even though I have mostly been quiet here. Now if this is not a typical example of serendipity and exemplary of the effect of all that we are stepping into in the Big Energy – where our frequency is felt first - then I do not know what is.

Closing

You could say I have come a long way, risen from the ashes, followed a calling, and stepped into my purpose. That I have become the person I once desired to be.

Along this journey, as I focused on my work, I have been single for a while now, particularly in the latter part of these last three years. During this time, I have abstained from sex, mostly without alcohol, and with plenty of quiet time for deep contemplation. There is no doubt that this solitude has sharpened my spiritual abilities. I have often pondered whether this was my fate, a purposeful path of spiritual work and solitude.

This journey has given me ample time to reflect, and at times I have accepted that this may be the role I am here to play.

To be honest, this feels bittersweet.

There is an aspect of me (my human) that longs for union with *my* person with an almost naive belief (that most of us have) that there is someone out there who, if we come together, will not diminish my spiritual abilities but enhance them. I imagine a union that is not just for our own joy, but one that serves a greater good in the world – as we go on our own sweet and rich adventures. With this hope in mind, years ago - I dabbled in online dating apps, but that path brought no joy to my soul.

I have created a beautiful home and foundation for myself and my son. I love what I do, and I finally feel at ease stepping into my Big Energy as I show up in the world. The publishing of this book marks another chapter of my journey, one where I feel ready to step into a new phase. A phase I am just beginning to be clear on, as I sit here in the mountains finishing this book.

I sense that the journey ahead will lead me through yet another rabbit hole, one where I must go deeper into healing my heart, for there is still more work to be done. It is a call to step further into all that I am and to embody my Big Energy in its fullest expression – whatever that may look like.

And that is the essence of Big Energy; it is about embracing the vastness of who we are, even when the path feels uncertain or lonely. It is about honouring both the solitude and the longing, the work and the love, the growth, and the surrender. Big Energy is not about fixing or achieving; it is about expanding, accepting, and living in alignment with our truest selves, even when we are still in the process of 'becoming.'

So, as you move forward from this point, I invite you to keep wearing your own Big Energy Pants, whatever that looks like for you. Continue to expand, explore, and honour the entirety of your journey. Remember, it is not about the destination; it is about showing up as your whole self, trusting that every step is leading you to an even deeper and more authentic version of you.

Here's to the next chapter, for all of us, one filled with growth, love, and the courage to embody our Big Energy.

A Last One from the Guides on The Potency of 'I Am'

'All things should be sacred. When you make your actions sacred you hold a container of energy with utmost reverence.

You yourself were made with sacredness. A body of energy forces with power to expand and contract as he or she pleases. However, when you start to treat yourself, or anything, without sacredness, you start to lose this energy and become a leaky container; sacredness comes from the reverence to upholding God's energy.

Without this intention, you cannot match the level of energy/vibration. Already when you say "I am" you are making a strong intention to be one with God; this pure energy of love that binds us altogether and it is all.

"I am" is the fruit of an awakened heart.

That you are one with all, for all, with the purest intentions, service, and above all - love.'

✳

Morning Practice: I am

Every morning before you get out of bed, you could start your day with a mindful recitation of 'I am' a few times.

Start with 21 times, perhaps, and watch how this energetically shifts your whole being and your day.

Whenever you feel lost or unsettled, bring your thoughts back to 'I am.'

Silently in your mind, recite the mantra 'I am' to bring yourself back home to your true state; whole, complete pure love.

A Parting Gift - Download the Gold Frequency Activation

The *Gold Frequency Activation* is a two-minute energetic journey designed to pull you into a higher dimensional space, raise your vibration, and align you with the energy of wealth, expansion, and clarity.

By tuning into the gold frequency, the energy of luxury, abundance, and feminine creation, and the frequency of 'I am' you are activating the version of you who already holds your vision. This is the space where big shifts, synchronicities, and effortless momentum happen.

You can access this here:

I hope this book, the downloads, practices, and activations serve you well on your journey forwards.

I am.

Together we are.

Our Journey Together: A Closing Note

As we come to the end of this book, I want you to pause for a moment and breathe in everything we've explored together.

We began with a question - **what if the missing piece isn't something you need to learn, but something you need to unlock?**

And so, we set out on a journey. A journey of **healing, transformation, and conscious creation.**

We peeled back the layers in **HEAL**, where you met yourself more deeply, faced the call to awaken, and explored what it means to truly **heal and build resilience.** You saw that your past does not define you, but **what you choose to do with it does.**

We then moved into **TRANSFORM**, where you gathered the tools to step into your power. You learned that self-love isn't just about bubble baths, it's about **self-worth, boundaries, and claiming space.** You discovered how to work with fear, doubt, and imposter syndrome, not as enemies, but as doorways to growth. And you tapped into the **energetic forces** that exist within and around you, learning to harness them in ways that bring ease instead of exhaustion.

Finally, we arrived at **CREATE**, where you were invited to step fully into **who you are meant to be.** To manifest with intention. To walk the path of your **true purpose** with clarity. To live **authentically** and redefine happiness, not as something you chase, but as something you cultivate.

Through every chapter, every story, and every moment of reflection, I hope you have felt one thing above all else: **you are powerful beyond measure.**

What Now?

This is not the end, this is the beginning.

The real journey starts here, in the quiet moments **after** you close this book. When you decide to take what you've learned and put it into practice.

So, what's next?

- **Start a ritual** - even if it's just one small thing each day that reconnects you to your Big Energy.
- **Get yourself a journal** - document your shifts, your insights, your breakthroughs. Let this book be the first entry in a new chapter of your life.
- **Surround yourself with energy that fuels you** - whether it's through people, environments, or the practices that light you up.
- **Commit to yourself** - whether that's investing in your growth, creating boundaries, or simply allowing yourself to receive.

And above all, **trust that you are ready.**

No more waiting. No more doubting.

It's time.

Time to step forward. Time to own your power. Time to step into your **Big Energy.**

And I, for one, cannot wait to see what you do next.

Access Free Resources & Tools

Start your journey with free resources – Dive into guided practices, energy tools, and powerful exercises to support your transformation. Access them all here: **https://innerpowergame.co.uk/big-energy-resources/**

With love and power,
Folake Balogun

About the Author

Folake Balogun is a mentor, guide, and activator who helps high-level leaders, CEOs, coaches, and entrepreneurs **expand their energy, impact, and wealth** in a way that feels deeply aligned.

Her journey wasn't always about mastering energy and transformation. For over a decade, she was behind the scenes; running an award-winning video production company that worked with names like **Tony Robbins and Selena Gomez.** On the surface, it seemed like a dream. But inside? **Burnout, exhaustion, and a deep longing for something more.**

Then came the turning point. **A brain tumour diagnosis, a spiritual awakening, and an undeniable pull toward a different way of living.** One that didn't involve pushing, proving, or constantly striving, but instead, **moving with power, attracting with ease, and creating with freedom.**

Now, she helps **ambitious leaders, entrepreneurs, and high-level individuals** step into their full power - offering **mentorship, strategy, and energetic mastery** in a way that goes beyond the ordinary. **From high-level business strategy to deep energy transformation,** she works with clients at bespoke levels - from private mentorship and consulting to done-for-you solutions.

Folake is available for:

- Speaking engagements
- Private mentorship & bespoke consulting
- Business, digital & energy transformation for CEOs & organisations
- Leadership coaching & energy mastery for coaches, mentors, and consultants

Beyond the Work:
Life, Nature & Freedom

A mother first, **Folake now enjoys a slower, more intentional life** after moving from the **hustle and bustle of London** to a more peaceful rural area in Hertfordshire. She finds joy in **long walks by the river, swimming, cycling, and escaping to nature whenever possible.** She retreats into the stillness of the land, but her **love for the sea and travel** often calls her to distant shores, reminding her that life is meant to be explored, both within and without.

Connect & Go Deeper

If *Big Energy Pants* resonated with you, let's continue this journey together.

Tune into the Inner Power Game Podcast – Listen to powerful conversations on energy, business, and creating success on your terms.

https://innerpowergame.co.uk/the-podcast/

Follow & Connect – Find me on https://www.instagram.com/folakebee for more insights, conversations, and behind-the-scenes moments.

This is your time. Let's make magic happen.

Printed in Dunstable, United Kingdom